# soprano
# musical theatre
## for classical singers

edited by richard walters

ISBN 978-1-4234-7417-3

7777 W. BLUEMOUND RD. P.O. BOX 13819 MILWAUKEE, WI 53213

For all works contained herein:
Unauthorized copying, arranging, adapting, recording, Internet posting, public performance,
or other distribution of the printed music in this publication is an infringement of copyright.
Infringers are liable under the law.

Visit Hal Leonard Online at
**www.halleonard.com**

# preface

Classical singers have been singing musical theatre since before the genre as we know it emerged, going back to its roots in operetta. Many well-known classical artists have performed and recorded musical theatre. A very partial list, and by no means comprehensive, might include José Carreras, Placido Domingo, Eileen Farrell, Renée Fleming, Jerry Hadley, Thomas Hampson, Marilyn Horne, Patrice Munsel, Luciano Pavarotti, Ezio Pinza, Leontyne Price, Samuel Ramey, Risë Stevens, Teresa Stratas, Kiri Te Kanawa, Bryn Terfel, Helen Traubel, Tatiana Troyanos, Deborah Voigt, Frederica von Stade. The list could go on almost indefinitely. If nothing else, that sampling of artists proves that there is not one specific classical voice type suited to singing musical theatre. Like opera, the genre accommodates a variety of vocal talents.

The time seems ripe, perhaps even overdue, for a series specifically addressing the needs of classical singers in musical theatre. Musical theatre is a common necessity in the repertory of any classical singer, at any level, from any English-speaking country, and particularly for North Americans. While opera singers get constant advice from teachers and coaches about individually suitable arias, such consideration of musical theatre literature is less common in classical circles. The truth is that in English-speaking countries, because of natural cultural familiarity, a typical audience may bring more discerning ears to performances of musical theatre than they bring to opera. A classical performer needs to respect that.

Specialty arrangements are always an option with a classical singer performing musical theatre, or standards from the "golden era," depending on the intent and performing situation. A singer who can find an excellent arrangement or excellent arranger to work with, perfectly suiting their voice, taste and temperament, is lucky indeed. This series does not address specialty arrangements, but rather a pure presentation of musical theatre repertory, in editions as the music was originally composed and performed in the context of a show.

## Original Keys?
Most times in this series songs are presented in original keys, but not always. In the Soprano, Tenor and Baritone/Bass volumes original keys are the norm, with a few explicit exceptions when vocal tessitura and range was better served by a transposition. The Mezzo-Soprano volume contains quite a few transpositions, primarily of soprano songs dropped down a bit to flatter lyric mezzo-sopranos. Also, a few belting range songs suitable for a classical mezzo-soprano have been transposed up into a better range.

## The Compilation
Essentially, the literature in this collection allows classical singers to sing with their classical core sound, without going into a completely different type of voice or production. However, a classical singer needs very much to adjust to musical theatre style, and realize that expressively communicating words, thoughts and meanings is paramount.

Many songs beyond those here could have appeared in these collections. There is ample literature out there that a classical singer might explore. These compilations are meant to present those songs thought most essential and useful to the most people. In each volume are some obvious choices for that voice type, but as compiler I also strove to include less trodden material that can potentially suit a classical voice well. As would be guessed, I avoided songs that are inherently written for and best performed by pop/rock or belting voices.

## Avoid the Pitfalls
Classical singers with technically solid, free and expressive voices can enhance any music they sing. Admittedly, classical tastes are sometimes different from theatre tastes. When theatre people complain about classical singers singing musical theatre, they usually mean some combination of the following:

- They are not actors. The performance has no depth, subtext or character.
- They make a performance far too much about the voice, and less about communicating the song.
- Their diction is poor and unclear.
- Their diction sounds artificial, and inappropriately disconnected from vernacular speech.
- They sing with a misplaced operatic sound that overwhelms the song.
- They are inexpressive, dull and bland, with no spontaneity.
- They sound square and rigid, and are maddeningly correct and exact to a fault.

It behooves any classical singer to consider those possible dangers in singing musical theatre, and to attempt to address them in the best way possible. This cannot be done by quickly throwing together a performance of a musical theatre song that someone accustomed to learning an opera aria perceives to be "easy." Unfortunately, that is too often the case. Preparation of a musical theatre song needs to be as insightful and diligent as when one prepares an aria. Because the technical vocal challenges usually are not as prominent or exposed in musical theatre, singers sometimes tend to think that songs from that genre need less preparation. Actually, they need as much preparation as it takes to make them sound completely natural and convincing.

The word "theatre" is the clue to musical theatre. This music needs to be approached theatrically, and made vivid to come to life. This is not at all a matter of singing louder. It involves connecting to the song and finding spontaneous, strong communication with an audience. The singer also needs to realize that almost all musical theatre is written with an assumption in mind: that the performer will bring personality and style to fill out the material beyond what is on the page. Classical singers do not always understand this.

**Choosing a Song**

Whether they have mastered the practical application of it or not, opera singers and those who aspire to it are aware that choice of aria is a crucial issue for an individual voice. Not all voices can sing Puccini, or Wagner, or Donizetti, or Handel, or Verdi. A singer learns over time, with some trial and error and input from various sources, what music best suits them. While vocal *fachs* are not at all defined in musical theatre, individual classical singers still need to be aware that some songs suit them better than others.

Some blessed singers have talents and voices that are so flexible that they seem to be able to do anything, from comedy to drama, from opera to art song to Broadway, from swing to contemporary pop/rock material. Such talents are very rare. If you are a classical singer who feels uncomfortable singing in any kind of popular music styles, even after working at it, and have a difficult time loosening up to any degree, then you should strategically chose musical theatre literature that is more closely aligned to classical music in its style.

Choose something that you like, that you sing well, and that fits you as would a custom-tailored suit. Take into account what you look like, your vocal instrument, your age, and your temperament as a performer. Most important, choose a song you believe in, one which expresses a character or emotions with which you can identify in a real way. Then be brave enough to express genuine emotion in a performance. Actors are trained to do that very thing, refined by technique. Somehow many classical singers keep real emotion at bay, as if it is an enemy to good singing. Those who can find a way to let emotion flow naturally will succeed best in musical theatre.

**Diction**

There is only space for a few words on this important and large topic. I believe that a classical singer would probably benefit from thinking of musical theatre diction as closely related to American speech (in most cases, since the bulk of musical theatre literature in these collections is American in origin). I think this is truer of musical theatre than of art song in English, which is comprised of the stylized language of poetry, or of opera in English, which needs a different emphasis. Speak the words of your musical theatre selection clearly and naturally, as a North American would in natural "standard" speech (noticing the infrequency of front dental consonants), and attempt to sing with the same diction, rather than moving into more elevated, rounded diction unrelated to everyday speech. Adjustments surely will need to be made for singing, and character songs may require special diction. But the point is natural expression. If you sound artificial and too formal for material that is written in the language of spoken American vernacular, as most musical theatre is, then you have not found the style of the song.

**Benefits**

There are clear benefits to a classical singer in thoroughly studying and preparing musical theatre repertory. It is very possible that one might find freedom of expression in musical theatre that has been elusive in opera arias, art song or oratorio. If this is the case, then the singer should ask, "Even though the musical style of opera or art song or oratorio is completely different from musical theatre, requiring more discipline and vocal consistency, how can I find the same degree of expression and communication that I find in musical theatre?"

I thank Joel Boyd for his help with these volumes, and assistant editor Joshua Parman for his diligence in helping me to complete the publications.

Richard Walters
Editor

# contents
## alphabetically by show

**THE BOYS FROM SYRACUSE**
- 1    Falling in Love with Love

**CAROUSEL**
- 10    Mister Snow
- 18    If I Loved You
- 22    What's the Use of Wond'rin'
- 26    You'll Never Walk Alone

**THE ENCHANTRESS**
- 28    Art Is Calling for Me

**FANNY**
- 34    I Have to Tell You

**FIORELLO!**
- 37    When Did I Fall in Love

**FLOWER DRUM SONG**
- 42    Love, Look Away

**FOLLIES**
- 50    One More Kiss

**GREY GARDENS**
- 45    Will You?

**INTO THE WOODS**
- 79    Children Will Listen

**THE KING AND I**
- 54    My Lord and Master
- 57    Hello, Young Lovers
- 62    We Kiss in a Shadow
- 66    I Have Dreamed

**KISMET**
- 72    Baubles, Bangles and Beads
- 76    And This Is My Beloved

**KISS ME, KATE**
- 84    So in Love

**LADY IN THE DARK**
- 90    My Ship

**LES MISÉRABLES**
- 88    In My Life

**THE LIGHT IN THE PIAZZA**
- 93    The Beauty Is

**ME AND JULIET**
- 100    No Other Love

**MERRILY WE ROLL ALONG**
- 108    Not a Day Goes By

**THE MOST HAPPY FELLA**
- 104    Somebody, Somewhere

**MUSIC IN THE AIR**
- 111    The Song Is You

**THE MUSIC MAN**
- 114    Goodnight, My Someone
- 118    My White Knight
- 122    Till There Was You

**MY FAIR LADY**
- 126    I Could Have Danced All Night
- 133    Show Me

**THE MYSTERY OF EDWIN DROOD**
- 138    Moonfall

**OKLAHOMA!**
- 148    Out of My Dreams

**110 IN THE SHADE**
- 141    Old Maid

**PHANTOM**
    154    This Place Is Mine

**THE PHANTOM OF THE OPERA**
    163    Think of Me
    170    Wishing You Were Somehow Here Again

**RAGS**
    174    Children of the Wind

**SHE LOVES ME**
    180    Will He Like Me?
    186    Dear Friend
    190    Vanilla Ice Cream

**SHOW BOAT**
    197    Make Believe
    202    Can't Help Lovin' Dat Man
    206    Bill

**1600 PENNSYLVANIA AVENUE**
    218    Take Care of This House

**THE SOUND OF MUSIC**
    209    The Sound of Music
    214    Climb Ev'ry Mountain

**SPRING IS HERE**
    222    With a Song in My Heart

**STREET SCENE**
    226    What Good Would the Moon Be?

**SWEENEY TODD**
    234    Green Finch and Linnet Bird

**SWEET ADELINE**
    231    Why Was I Born?

**TWO BY TWO**
    240    The Golden Ram

**WEST SIDE STORY**
    248    I Feel Pretty
    255    Somewhere

**WICKED**
    258    Let Us Be Glad

## contents
*alphabetically by song title*

| Page | Song | Show |
|---|---|---|
| 76 | And This Is My Beloved | *Kismet* |
| 28 | Art Is Calling for Me | *The Enchantress* |
| 72 | Baubles, Bangles and Beads | *Kismet* |
| 93 | The Beauty Is | *The Light in the Piazza* |
| 206 | Bill | *Show Boat* |
| 202 | Can't Help Lovin' Dat Man | *Show Boat* |
| 174 | Children of the Wind | *Rags* |
| 79 | Children Will Listen | *Into the Woods* |
| 214 | Climb Ev'ry Mountain | *The Sound of Music* |
| 186 | Dear Friend | *She Loves Me* |
| 1 | Falling in Love with Love | *The Boys from Syracuse* |
| 240 | The Golden Ram | *Two by Two* |
| 114 | Goodnight, My Someone | *The Music Man* |
| 234 | Green Finch and Linnet Bird | *Sweeney Todd* |
| 57 | Hello, Young Lovers | *The King and I* |
| 126 | I Could Have Danced All Night | *My Fair Lady* |
| 248 | I Feel Pretty | *West Side Story* |
| 66 | I Have Dreamed | *The King and I* |
| 34 | I Have to Tell You | *Fanny* |
| 18 | If I Loved You | *Carousel* |
| 88 | In My Life | *Les Misérables* |
| 258 | Let Us Be Glad | *Wicked* |
| 42 | Love, Look Away | *Flower Drum Song* |
| 197 | Make Believe | *Show Boat* |
| 10 | Mister Snow | *Carousel* |
| 138 | Moonfall | *The Mystery of Edwin Drood* |
| 54 | My Lord and Master | *The King and I* |
| 90 | My Ship | *Lady in the Dark* |
| 118 | My White Knight | *The Music Man* |
| 100 | No Other Love | *Me and Juliet* |
| 108 | Not a Day Goes By | *Merrily We Roll Along* |
| 141 | Old Maid | *110 in the Shade* |
| 50 | One More Kiss | *Follies* |
| 148 | Out of My Dreams | *Oklahoma!* |
| 133 | Show Me | *My Fair Lady* |
| 84 | So in Love | *Kiss Me, Kate* |
| 104 | Somebody, Somewhere | *The Most Happy Fella* |
| 255 | Somewhere | *West Side Story* |
| 111 | The Song Is You | *Music in the Air* |
| 209 | The Sound of Music | *The Sound of Music* |
| 218 | Take Care of This House | *1600 Pennsylvania Avenue* |
| 163 | Think of Me | *The Phantom of the Opera* |
| 154 | This Place Is Mine | *Phantom* |
| 122 | Till There Was You | *The Music Man* |
| 190 | Vanilla Ice Cream | *She Loves Me* |
| 62 | We Kiss in a Shadow | *The King and I* |
| 226 | What Good Would the Moon Be? | *Street Scene* |
| 22 | What's the Use of Wond'rin' | *Carousel* |
| 37 | When Did I Fall in Love | *Fiorello!* |
| 231 | Why Was I Born? | *Sweet Adeline* |
| 180 | Will He Like Me? | *She Loves Me* |
| 45 | Will You? | *Grey Gardens* |
| 170 | Wishing You Were Somehow Here Again | *The Phantom of the Opera* |
| 222 | With a Song in My Heart | *Spring Is Here* |
| 26 | You'll Never Walk Alone | *Carousel* |

# notes on the shows and songs

## THE BOYS FROM SYRACUSE

### Falling in Love with Love

Music by Richard Rodgers
Lyrics by Lorenz Hart
Book by George Abbott
Opened on Broadway 23 November 1938 for an initial run of 235 performances

The idea for *The Boys from Syracuse* began when Rodgers and Hart, while working on another show, were discussing the fact that no one had yet done a musical based on a play by Shakespeare. Hart's choice was *The Comedy of Errors*, chiefly because his actor brother Teddy Hart was always being confused with a better known comic actor, Jimmy Savo. The plot is a whirlwind of complex silliness and mistaken identity set in ancient Mediterranean locales. Accompanied by his servant Dromio, Antipholus of Syracuse journeys to Ephesus in search of his long lost twin brother, Antipholus of Ephesus. By an amazing coincidence of plot, Dromio's twin brother, also called Dromio, is servant to Antipholus of Ephesus. Complications arise when the wives of the Ephesians, Adriana and her servant Luce, mistake the two strangers from Syracuse for their husbands. Yet Adriana's sister, Luciana, falls in love with the Syrcause merchant, and all somehow ends happily. An Off-Broadway revival, more successful than the original Broadway run, opened in 1963; a London production opened later that same year. A film adaptation of the musical was released in 1940.

Near the top of the show Adriana, wife of Antipholus of Ephesus, sings **"Falling in Love with Love"** to her sister as they sew. Her husband neglects her and instead spends his attention on courtesans. The song is a breezy description of her troubled marriage.

## CAROUSEL

### Mister Snow
### If I Loved You
### What's the Use of Wond'rin'
### You'll Never Walk Alone

Music by Richard Rodgers
Lyrics and Book by Oscar Hammerstein II
Opened on Broadway 19 April 1945 for an initial run of 890 performances

The collaborators of *Oklahoma!* chose Ferenc Molnar's play *Liliom* as the basis for their second show together. Oscar Hammerstein shifted Molnar's Budapest locale to a late 19th-century fishing village in New England. The two principal roles are Billy Bigelow, a shiftless carnival barker, and Julie Jordan, an ordinary mill worker. This is not merely a simple boy meets girl plot, but contains a predominant theme of tragedy throughout most of the play. Rodgers always cited *Carousel* as the score he was most proud of in his long career. Julie and Carrie Pipperidge, a friend and fellow mill worker, stroll by the sea shore near a carnival, where Julie has exchanged some familiarity with the carousel barker, Billy, whom she does not know. Carrie confesses her own romance with **"Mister Snow."** Billy comes into the scene. Carrie reminds Julie that if they are seen out in the evening they will lose their jobs at Mr. Bascombe's mill, and Carrie leaves. Mr. Bascombe himself comes along, with a policeman, and offers to take Julie home so that she can keep her job. She refuses and is fired. Left alone with Billy and feeling at sea, Julie expresses the mysterious attraction she feels for him in **"If I Loved You."** (The song is first sung by Julie in this extended duet scene, then by Billy.) The song is the writers' device to instantly create undeniable romance between characters who have only just met. Oscar Hammerstein used a similar strategy in "Make Believe" from *Show Boat* (1927).

Julie and Billy marry. At a clambake some months later a whaler tries to seduce Carrie. Unfortunately, Enoch Snow discovers her in what appears to be a compromising position and ends their engagement. Carrie's friends try to comfort her, saying all men are bad. Julie, who by now has endured Billy's hotheaded moods and probably his abuse, reflects simply that all that matters is that "he's your feller and you love him" in **"What's the Use of Wond'rin'."** After learning he is to be a father, and realizing he needs money, with an accomplice Billy attempts a robbery, and stabs himself and dies after being cornered by the police. Nettie Fowler, the maternal figure in the show, comforts Julie with **"You'll Never Walk Alone."** Julie has a daughter, and years later at the girl's high school graduation Billy's spirit appears and comforts both of them while **"You'll Never Walk Alone"** is reprised.

The musical was produced in London in 1950. A film version was released in 1956. A prominent Broadway revival opened in 1994, a production that originated at the Royal National Theatre in London.

## THE ENCHANTRESS

### Art Is Calling for Me

Music by Victor Herbert
Lyrics and Book by Harry B. Smith
Opened on Broadway 19 October 1911 for an initial run of 112 performances

The Irish born Victor Herbert (1859–1924) was the most successful American composer of his time. He and his mother moved to Germany in 1866 when she married a German physician, and he received his musical training in that country, becoming an excellent cellist. Herbert's wife, a soprano, was engaged by the Metropolitan Opera, and he came along to New York, soon to be at the center of the city's musical life as a cellist and conductor. He began composing operettas in 1894 and wrote 40 such works in the next 30 years. The plots of these pieces are formulaic by today's standards and often negligible. The only one performed regularly is *Babes in Toyland* (1903). *The Red Mill* (1906) was successfully revived on Broadway in 1945 and was Herbert's biggest hit in his time.

*The Enchantress* takes place in the fictional eastern European country of Zergovia. A prima donna, Vivien Savary, is persuaded by a scheming cabinet minister to seduce the ruler, Prince Ivan, who will be forced to abdicate his throne if he marries a commoner. Vivien and Prince Ivan fall in love, but before the abdication plot happens it is discovered that the Vivien has royal blood. All ends happily. There are six princesses among the supporting players, one of whom is Princess Stellina, who sings her only solo in the show, accompanied by chorus, with **"Art Is Calling for Me,"** sometimes called "The Prima Donna Song," a longtime favorite of sopranos.

## FANNY
### I Have to Tell You

Music and Lyrics by Harold Rome
Book by S.N. Behrman and Joshua Logan
Opened on Broadway 4 November 1954 for an initial run of 888 performances

Marcel Pagnol's French film trilogy, *Marius*, *Fanny*, and *César*, were combined into one tale as the basis for *Fanny*, the musical. It is a soaring, emotional score. Set in Marseilles, Fanny, whose father owns a fish shop, is secretly in love with Marius. One night she can no longer hide her feelings, worried that Marius is taken with another girl, and bursts into the bar owned by Marius' father as Marius is closing for the night. She passionately confesses to him her feelings in **"I Have to Tell You."** He replies that he is leaving the next day for a five-year commitment as a sailor. Fanny and Marius make love, and she bids him a sad farewell. Months later she discovers she is pregnant. Parnisse, an old widower, has pursued Fanny in the past. In desperation she seeks him, and tells him the truth. Parnisse is thrilled with the prospect of an heir, and marries Fanny to raise her child as his own. Marius learns of his son and returns on the boy's first birthday demanding both Fanny and his child. His father, César, convinces him that Panisse has the more rightful claim. Years go by. At age 13 the boy longs to go to sea like his father, and runs away to join him. This is too much for the now ill and aged Panisse, who dictates a letter to Marius offering him Fanny's hand in marriage. Marius brings the boy back to fulfill Panisse's dying wish. *Fanny* opened in London in 1956. A non-musical film of *Fanny* was released in 1961; none of the songs were included.

## FIORELLO!
### When Did I Fall in Love

Music by Jerry Bock
Lyrics by Sheldon Harnick
Book by Jerome Weidman and George Abbott
Opened on Broadway 23 November 1959 for an initial run of 795 performances

New York's favorite mayor, Fiorello LaGuardia (1882–1947), was a peppery, pugnacious reformer whose larger-than-life personality readily lent itself to depiction on the musical stage. He served three terms in the city's highest office, 1934–1945. *Fiorello!* covers the period in LaGuardia's life before he became mayor. It begins with his surprise election to congress prior to World War I. **"When Did I Fall in Love"** is sung by his adoring wife after he strides off to work at Capitol Hill. To make the song a little less plot specific, in this edition as editor I have made a cut of the first section of the introduction/verse. The cut lyrics are "There he goes, my congressman. Starting his day hurrying right to a fight. There he goes, Sir Galahad, galloping off riding his white Willie's knight." (The complete verse appears in *The Singer's Musical Theatre Anthology, Soprano Volume 2*.) As editor, I have also suggested that a performance might skip the verse entirely, and begin with measure 25. *Fiorello!* had the distinction of being the third musical to win the Pulitzer Prize in Drama, joining the ranks of *Of Thee I Sing* and *South Pacific*.

## FLOWER DRUM SONG
### Love, Look Away

Music by Richard Rodgers
Lyrics by Oscar Hammerstein II
Book by Oscar Hammerstein II and Joseph Fields
Opened on Broadway 1 December 1958 for an initial run of 600 performances

It was librettist Joseph Fields who first secured the rights to C.Y. Lee's novel (*The Flower Drum Song*, published in 1957), and then approached Rodgers and Hammerstein to join him as collaborators. To dramatize the conflict between the traditionalist older Chinese-Americans living in San Francisco and their thoroughly Americanized offspring, the musical tells the story of Mei Li, a timid "picture bride" from China, who arrives to fulfill her contract to marry night-club owner Sammy Fong. Sammy, however, prefers dancer Linda Low, who obviously enjoys being a girl, and the problem is resolved when Sammy's friend Wang Ta discovers that Mei Li is really the bride for him. In Act I Wang Ta's childhood friend Helen Chao, a seamstress, sings of her unrequited love for Ta in **"Love, Look Away."** (The role of Helen, originally for soprano, was transposed down into a belting range for the 2002 Broadway revival.) *Flower Drum Song* opened in London in 1960. A film version of the musical was released in 1961.

## FOLLIES

### One More Kiss

Music and Lyrics by Stephen Sondheim
Book by James Goldman
Opened on Broadway 4 April 1971 for an initial run of 522 performances

Taking place at a 1971 reunion of former Ziegfeld Follies-type showgirls of the 1930s at the soon to be demolished Weismann Theatre, the musical deals with the reality of life as contrasted with the unreality of the theatre. It explores this theme through the lives of two couples, the upper class, unhappy Phyllis and Benjamin Stone, and the middle-class, unhappy Sally and Buddy Plummer. *Follies* also depicts these four as they were in their pre-marital youth. Because the show is about the past, and often in flashback, using rather cinematic devices, Sondheim purposefully stylized some of songs in the score to evoke some of the theatre's great composers and lyricists of the 1920s and '30s. Such is the case with **"One More Kiss,"** which is a duet in the show between Heidi Schiller, a retired operetta singer, and her young self. It has been adapted as a solo for this edition. A revised version of the show was presented in London in 1987, with some songs replaced with new numbers. *Follies* was given two concert performances in 1985 at Avery Fisher Hall in New York with an all star cast, resulting in the most revered recording of the show. Retired Metropolitan Opera star Licia Albanese was "old Heidi" and Erie Mills was "young Heidi" in this cast recording of **"One More Kiss."**

## GREY GARDENS

### Will You?

Music by Scott Frankel
Lyrics by Michael Korie
Book by Doug Wright
Opened Off-Broadway 10 February 2006
Opened on Broadway 2 November 2006 for an initial a run of 307 performances

*Grey Gardens*, the musical, is based on *Grey Gardens*, the 1975 film documentary, about an eccentric mother and her equally eccentric daughter. Both remain for decades in a crumbling mansion on Long Island in East Hampton, New York. After a Prologue, Act I of the musical speculates on the past of the principal characters as they were in July, 1941: 47-year-old mother Edith Bouvier Beale, aunt to Jacqueline Bouvier (later Kennedy Onassis), and her 21-year-old daughter Edith "Little Edie" Bouvier Beale. Their mansion home is refined and cultivated. Little Edie is in a relationship with Joseph Kennedy, Jr. (older brother of the president), but her mother sabotages it. The engagement is off, though the guests are assembled for the party to celebrate it. The mother Edith, a singer, glosses over any trouble, instead taking center stage and performing "one of our all-time favorites," the wistful **"Will You?"** It is written in the style of sentimental operetta of the 1910s and '20s. The song becomes predictive about her daughter, who remains with her mother. In Act II of the musical, set in 1973 and most closely based on the documentary, the 79-year-old Edith, and her 56-year-old unmarried daughter Little Edie are faded aristocrats living in filth and ruin, isolated from the world, drifting in time. Their relationship is complex and co-dependent. On Broadway Christine Ebersole played the mother in Act I, and the daughter in Act II.

## INTO THE WOODS

### Children Will Listen

Music and Lyrics by Stephen Sondheim
Book by James Lapine
Opened on Broadway 5 November 1987 for an initial run of 765 performances

*Into the Woods* brought together for the second time the Pulitzer Prize winning team of Lapine and Sondheim. They turned to children's fairy tales as their subject. The book of *Into the Woods* often focuses on the darker, grotesque aspects of these stories, but by highlighting them, it touches on the themes of interpersonal relationships, death, and what we pass on to our children. Act I begins with the familiar "once upon a time" stories, and masterfully interweaves the plots of Snow White, Little Red Riding Hood, Cinderella, Jack and the Beanstalk, Rapunzel, a Baker and his Wife and others. Act II concerns what happens after "happily ever after," as reality sets in, and the fairy tale plots dissolve into more human stories. At the end of the show, the Baker quietly tells his infant son the story of the boy's birth, and the morals learned. The Witch sings **"Children Will Listen"** (later joined by the whole ensemble). Though the role of the Witch is principally for a belter, **"Children Will Listen"** is in a more soprano range, and certainly can be successfully sung by a classical singer. *Into the Woods* opened in London in 1990.

# THE KING AND I

**My Lord and Master**
**Hello, Young Lovers**
**We Kiss in a Shadow**
**I Have Dreamed**

Music by Richard Rodgers
Lyrics and Book by Oscar Hammerstein II
Opened on Broadway 29 March 1951 for an initial run of 1246 performances

The musical is adapted from Margaret Landon's semi-fictionalized biographical 1944 novel, *Anna and the King of Siam,* which was based on memoirs of Anna Leonowens (1831–1915). The story is set in Bangkok, Siam, in the early 1860s, in and around the king's palace. Anna Leonowens, a widowed Englishwoman, arrives with her young son to begin the post of schoolteacher to the Siamese royal children. She has frequent clashes with the monarch but eventually comes to exert great influence on him, particularly in creating a more democratic society for his people. Tuptim, a young Burmese woman presented to the King of Siam as the latest addition to his collection of wives (a gift from the Prince of Burma) arrives escorted by courtier Lun Tha. Tuptim and Lun Tha have fallen in love. The King receives his new wife with little ceremony, and leaves her alone to regard her dire circumstances in **"My Lord and Master."** (Originally in a soprano range, the role of Tuptim was transposed to a belter range for the 1996 Broadway revival.) **"Hello, Young Lovers"** is sung by Anna as she reflects sympathetically on the relationship between Tuptim and Lun Tha and remembers the love of her deceased husband. (It has been transposed up in this edition to a more comfortable classical soprano range.) Lun Tha and Tuptim have been meeting in secret with Anna as lookout. The threat of the King's wrath prompts them to sing **"We Kiss in a Shadow."** In Act II the lovers Lun Tha and Tuptim have decided to escape the court of Siam, risking great danger, and sing **"I Have Dreamed"** in anticipation of being away together. Both duets (**"We Kiss in a Shadow," "I Have Dreamed"**) have been adapted as solos for this edition. *The King and I* played in London in 1953. A film version of the musical was released in 1956.

# KISMET

**Baubles, Bangles and Beads**
**And This Is My Beloved**

Music and Lyrics by Robert Wright and George Forrest
The score is based on music by Alexander Borodin
Book by Charles Lederer and Luther Davis
Opened on Broadway 3 December 1953 for an initial run of 583 performances

The story of *Kismet* was adapted from Edward Knoblock's play, first presented in New York in 1911. The music of *Kismet* was adapted from themes by Alexander Borodin in such works as the "Polovetzian Dances" from the opera *Prince Igor*. The action of the musical occurs within a 24-hour period, in and around ancient Baghdad. A poor, scheming, gypsy-like Public Poet assumes the identity of Hajj the beggar and gets into all sorts of Arabian Nights adventures. His conniving gets him elevated to the position of emir of Baghdad, and as a result, his beautiful daughter Marsinah weds the handsome young Caliph. In the lead up to **"Baubles, Bangles and Beads"** in Act I Marsinah has previously been sent by her father to steal oranges for their breakfast from stall merchants in the bazaar. The fruit vendor, victim of her theft, pursues her, and her father steps in just in time to give the vendor some money just craftily acquired. The Poet gives Marsinah some cash, and she strolls the bazaar, looking at the jewelry and singing **"Baubles, Bangles and Beads,"** accompanied by ensemble. The dashing Caliph first spots her at the bazaar. Marsinah later sings **"And This Is My Beloved"** to the young Prince Caliph, her new husband. *Kismet* had a successful run in London, opening in 1955. A film version was released in 1955. A 1991 studio recording featured Samuel Ramey in the role of the Poet, soprano Ruth Ann Swensen as Marsinah, and Jerry Hadley as Caliph.

# KISS ME, KATE

**So in Love**

Music and Lyrics by Cole Porter
Book by Samuel and Bella Spewack
Opened on Broadway 30 December 1948 for an initial run of 1077 performances

The genesis of Cole Porter's longest running musical occurred in 1935 when producer Saint Subber, then a stagehand for the Theatre Guild's production of Shakespeare's *The Taming of the Shrew*, became aware that its stars, Alfred Lunt and Lynn Fontanne, quarreled almost as much in private as did the characters in the play. The entire action of *Kiss Me, Kate* occurs backstage and onstage at Ford's Theatre, Baltimore, during a pre-Broadway tryout tour of a musical version of *The Taming of the Shrew*. The main plot concerns the egotistical actor-producer Fred Graham and his temperamental ex-wife Lilli Vanessi. In Act I Lilli receives flowers in her dressing room from her ex-husband, a replica of her wedding bouquet, and realizes that even though she finds him infuriating she still loves him, singing **"So in Love."** Fred actually intended the flowers for another lady in the cast, Lois, which Lilli later learns, creating fury. Like Shakespeare's Petruchio and Kate, Fred and Lilli fight and go through much misunderstanding, with lots of other shenanigans from others thrown into the story, before they make up and eventually demonstrate their enduring affection for one other. One of the chief features of the score is the skillful way Cole Porter combined his own musical world ("So in Love," "Too Darn Hot," "Why Can't You Behave?", etc.) with a Shakespearean world (songs such as "I Hate Men" and "Where Is the Life That Late I Led?"). *Kiss Me, Kate* opened in London in 1950. A film version (without the comma in the title) was released in 1953.

## LADY IN THE DARK
### My Ship

Music by Kurt Weill
Lyrics by Ira Gershwin
Book by Moss Hart
Opened on Broadway 23 January 1941 for an initial run of 162 performances

Moss Hart initially intended *Lady in the Dark* to be a straight play, but after deciding to make it a star vehicle for Gertrude Lawrence, he hired Weill and Gershwin to turn it into a musical. Fiercely driven *Allure* magazine editor Liza Elliot is working too hard. Something is beginning to consume her, causing her sleepless nights, bouts of depression, and unproductiveness at work. She decides to see a psychoanalyst for help. He begins to open up her world of dreams to find out what is the matter. Much of the show is the manifestation of these flights of fancy, as Liza wrestles with her problems. The song **"My Ship,"** which she learned as a child, emerges in the sessions, but now only lies incomplete on the fringes of her memory. In the end, Liza is cured of her problems, due in large part to meeting Charley Johnson, with whom she falls in love when he is able to complete the song **"My Ship"** for her, which she then sings. With the exception of **"My Ship,"** the musical numbers are sung only during the elaborate dream sequences Liza describes to her doctor. The 1944 movie adaptation starred Ginger Rogers.

## LES MISÉRABLES
### In My Life

Music by Claude-Michel Schönberg
Lyrics by Herbert Kretzmer and Alain Boublil
Original French Text by Alain Boublil and Jean-Marc Natel
Opened in Paris September 1980 for an initial run of 3 months
Expanded and rewritten English version opened in London 8 October 1985
Opened on Broadway 12 March 1987 New York for an initial run of 6680 performances

This pop-opera epic was one of the defining musicals of the 1980s, distilling the drama from the 1200 page Victor Hugo novel of social injustice and the plight of the downtrodden (the "miserable ones" of the title). The original Parisian version contained only a few songs; many more were added when the show opened in London. Thus, most of the show's songs were originally performed in English. The dense plot is too rich to encapsulate, but centers on Jean Valjean, a prisoner sentenced to years of hard labor for stealing a loaf of bread for his starving family. He escapes and tries to start a new life, but soon finds himself hunted by the relentless Javert. The pursuit continues for years, across a tapestry of 19th century France that includes an armed uprising against the government, in which Valjean takes a heroic part. Along the way he acquires an adopted daughter, Cosette, who grows into young womanhood and attracts the attention of the handsome revolutionary Marius, and the envy of a street urchin rival, Eponine. The song **"In My Life"** gives Valjean and the young people a chance to wonder what each of them truly means to the other. It begins as Cosette's solo before becoming an ensemble.

## THE LIGHT IN THE PIAZZA
### The Beauty Is

Music and Lyrics by Adam Guettel
Book by Craig Lucas, based on the novella of the same name by Elizabeth Spencer
Opened on Broadway 18 April 2005 for an initial run of 504 performances

Finding inspiration in the same country as his grandfather Richard Rodgers' *Do I Hear a Waltz?*, Adam Guettel's *The Light in the Piazza* follows Americans abroad in Italy. The story, after a novella by Elizabeth Spencer, concerns Margaret, a wealthy North Carolinian mother, and her beautiful, childlike 26-year-old daughter, Clara, on extended vacation in Florence and Rome in the summer of 1953. Soon after their arrival in Florence, through a chance encounter Clara meets Fabrizio, a 20-year-old Italian man who speaks little English. Though there is a spark between them, Margaret protectively takes Clara away. As Clara strolls among the great art in the Uffizi Gallery, the paintings speak to her about herself, Italy, and her romantic yearnings as she sings **"The Beauty Is."** Fabrizio is determined, and with the help of his father, finally is able to spend time with Clara, though Margaret continues to attempt to discourage the romance. Margaret finally reveals the reason for her concern: due to being kicked in the head as a child by a pony, Clara has had arrested mental and emotional development. Margaret takes Clara to Rome to get her away from Fabrizio, but Clara's feelings for him remain fervent, and after much struggle she convinces her mother not to object to their marriage. Other obstacles emerge. Finally, just before the wedding Clara says to her mother that she cannot bear to leave her, but Margaret reassures her that she can. A non-musical film adaptation of the novella was released in 1962.

## ME AND JULIET
### No Other Love

Music by Richard Rodgers
Lyrics and Book by Oscar Hammerstein II
Opened on Broadway 28 May 1953 for an initial run of 358 performances

With an original book by Oscar Hammerstein II, *Me and Juliet* is a backstage musical comedy that takes place in and around the theatre where the musical, *Me and Juliet*, in a Broadway try-out run, is playing. Scenes and songs between the characters in the company are interspersed with scenes and songs from the show within the show. **"No Other Love"** is sung by Jeanie, a chorus singer in the show, in love with Larry, an assistant stage manager. The melody was adapted by Richard Rodgers from his score for the 1952 television documentary series *Victory at Sea*.

## MERRILY WE ROLL ALONG

### Not a Day Goes By

Music and Lyrics by Stephen Sondheim
Book by George Furth
Opened on Broadway 16 November 1981 for an initial run of 16 performances

Founded on the George S. Kaufman-Moss Hart play of the same name, *Merrily We Roll Along* has an innovative concept of telling its tale backwards, from 1976 when Franklin Shepard is a rich, famous, but morally compromised producer of formulaic movies, to his earlier days as a talented and optimistic Broadway composer working with his true friends Mary and Charley, to his idealistic youth when he graduated from high school in 1957. Near the end of Act I the story is now in 1966. Frank's wife Beth is divorcing him after he is caught in adultery. They are in a custody battle over their son. She sings **"Not a Day Goes By"** over her mixed feelings for Frank which she cannot escape. The song appears again in Act II six years earlier, with more romantic and hopeful lyrics, at their wedding. The role of Beth, originally for soprano, was transposed down into a belting range in the revised version of the musical.

## THE MOST HAPPY FELLA

### Somebody, Somewhere

Music, Lyrics and Book by Frank Loesser
Opened on Broadway 3 May 1956 for an initial run of 676 performances

Adapted from Sidney Howard's Pulitzer Prize-winning play, *They Knew What They Wanted*, *The Most Happy Fella* was a particularly ambitious, near operatic work for the Broadway theatre, with more than thirty separate musical numbers including arias, duets, trios, quartets, choral pieces, and recitatives. Antonio Esposito, an aging Napa Valley vineyard owner, proposes to a lonely San Francisco waitress, Rosabella, by leaving a letter for her in the diner. (Her real name is Amy, but Tony calls her Rosabella, and that is the name of the role for almost the entire show.) Rosabella has no idea who wrote the letter, but is moved, singing **"Somebody, Somewhere."** She and Tony begin a correspondence of letters. Rosabella has sent her picture and asks Tony for his. Embarrassed at the idea of sending a photograph of himself, he gets the idea of taking a picture of Joe, his handsome foreman. Joe does not know that Tony is sending it to Rosabella. She comes to Napa Valley after agreeing to marry Tony, and after meeting Joe quickly learns the truth about Tony sending a false picture of himself. Rosabella is shocked and upset, but also homeless with no money. Tony is in an automobile accident and, believing he may not live, persuades Rosabella to marry him immediately. She is very hesitant but agrees. After her wedding she is very upset, and Joe comforts her, which turns into lovemaking. Rosabella settles into life on the farm, though she and Joe are both tortured with guilt about their tryst on the night of Rosabella's marriage to Tony. Though still bandaged up and in a wheel chair, Tony is beginning to recover from his injuries. He apologizes to Rosabella for sending Joe's picture. Tony and Rosabella agree to attempt to start anew with one another. She grows to love Tony over time, but the couple has not consummated their relationship. Rosabella learns she is pregnant with Joe's child. She tells Tony the truth and he angrily throws her out. Tony threatens to kill Joe, but Joe leaves alone. There is reconciliation and the vintner persuades Rosabella to return home with him and offers to raise the unborn child as his own. *The Most Happy Fella* opened in London in 1960.

## MUSIC IN THE AIR

### The Song Is You

Music by Jerome Kern
Lyrics and Book by Oscar Hammerstein II
Opened on Broadway 8 November 1932 for an initial run of 342 performances

A "show within a show," *Music in the Air* reunited *Show Boat* writers Jerome Kern and Oscar Hammerstein. In the small Bavarian town of Edendorf, a music teacher and aspiring composer, Walther, begins a trek to Munich to try to get his songs published. He is joined by his daughter, Sieglinde, and her soon-to-be sweetheart Karl. Once in Munich they become mixed up in the middle of an operetta production and a rocky relationship between the diva Frieda, and her lover, the librettist/impresario Bruno. Outraged by the attention Bruno gives young Sieglinde, Frieda storms out of the production, and attempts to take the handsome Karl with her. Undaunted by the chaos surrounding his operetta, librettist Bruno continually tries to win the heart of Sieglinde, as in the duet **"The Song Is You"** (here adapted in this edition as a solo). The young country girl ends up being cast in the lead role, but against expectations in musical theatre, she doesn't have the skills to save the show! Father, daughter and Karl end up back in Edendorf to a happy ending of published songs and young love. A movie version was made in 1934, with Gloria Swanson in the diva's role. **"The Song Is You"** is representative of a late operetta style in the United States, near the end of the genre's popularity. Frank Sinatra was particularly fond of **"The Song Is You,"** and recorded and regularly performed a signature swing arrangement of it.

## THE MUSIC MAN

### Goodnight, My Someone
### My White Knight
### Till There Was You

Music, Lyrics and Book by Meredith Willson
Opened on Broadway 19 December 1957 for an initial run of 1375 performances

With *The Music Man*, Meredith Willson recaptured the innocent charm of the Middle America he knew growing up in an Iowa town. It is around the Fourth of July, 1912, in River City, Iowa, and "Professor" Harold Hill, a traveling salesman of musical instruments, has arrived to con the citizens into believing that he can teach the town's children how to play in a marching band. But instead of skipping town before the instruments are to arrive, as is his usual routine, Hill remains because of the love of a good woman, librarian and piano teacher Marian Paroo. The story ends with the children, though barely able to produce any kind of a recognizable musical sound with Hill's "think system," being hailed by their proud parents. Early in the story, just after Hill and Marian have met, and she has stubbornly attempted to ignore him, she sits on her front porch in the evening and sings her wish on the evening star about the man she dreams about in **"Goodnight, My Someone."** The next day Marian's mother, who likes Hill, attempts to learn why her daughter is not interested in him. She replies with her description of her ideal man (Hill clearly falls short of ideal in her mind), in **"My White Knight."** (Parts of the song were retained, and others replaced in the new song "Being in Love," created for the film version of the musical.) By the end of the musical Harold and Marian can no longer deny their love for one another in **"Till There Was You."** *The Music Man* opened in London in 1961. The film adaptation of the musical was released in 1962.

## MY FAIR LADY

### I Could Have Danced All Night
### Show Me

Music by Frederick Loewe
Lyrics and Book by Alan Jay Lerner
Opened on Broadway 15 March 1956 for an initial run of 2717 performances

The most celebrated musical of the 1950s began as an idea of Hungarian film producer Garbiel Pascal, who devoted the last two years of his life to trying to find writers to adapt George Bernard Shaw's play, *Pygmalion*, into a stage musical. The team of Lerner and Loewe also saw the possibilities, particularly when they realized that they could use most of the original dialogue and simply expand the action. They were also scrupulous in maintaining the Shavian flavor in their songs, most apparent in such pieces as "A Hymn to Him," "Why Can't the English?," "Show Me," and "Without You." Shaw's concern with class distinction and his belief that barriers would fall if all Englishmen would learn to speak properly was conveyed through a story about Eliza Doolittle, a scruffy and uneducated flower seller in Covent Garden, who takes speech lessons from Professor Henry Higgins (Rex Harrison in the original cast) so that she might qualify for the position of a florist in a shop. At first her progress is slow and frustrating. Finally one evening she is able to please the professor with proper pronunciation for the first time, and in his glee he dances with her. Her head spinning with giddiness, she can find no rest in her room later and sings **"I Could Have Danced All Night,"** despite the urgings of the servants for her to sleep. Higgins uses as a final test of her transformation a grand embassy ball, where Eliza succeeds so well that she is believed to be a princess. Insulted after being ignored as Higgins and his friend Colonel Pickering congratulate one another, she leaves his house in a rage, encountering Freddy, a penniless, foppish sap in love with her. He goes on with his romantic drivel and in a burst of emotion she sings **"Show Me."** Freddy is no match for the fiery Eliza. Higgins realizes that he has fallen in love with her. After swallowing a bit of his chauvinistic pride, Eliza gently returns to him.

*My Fair Lady* opened in London in 1958 with the same principals from the Broadway original cast. Harrison and Audrey Hepburn (whose singing was dubbed by Marni Nixon) costarred in the 1964 film version. It was a controversy at the time that Julie Andrews, the original Broadway Eliza, was not cast in the film. Aspiring Elizas will be interested in seeing the 1938 British film *Pygmalion*.

## THE MYSTERY OF EDWIN DROOD

### Moonfall

Music, Lyrics and Book by Rupert Holmes
Opened on Broadway 2 December 1985 for an initial run of 608 performances

The musical is adapted from a novel left unfinished by Charles Dickens upon his death in 1870. Since in the incomplete story there were no clues as to Drood's murderer, or even if a murder had been committed, Holmes decided to let the audience provide the show's ending by voting how it turns out. The writer's second major decision was to offer the musical as if it were being performed by an acting company at London's Music Hall Royale in 1873, drawing on British music hall and pantomime styles of the period. Rosa Budd is an orphan and Edwin Drood's fiancée, a betrothal arranged by their now dead fathers. (Edwin Drood is a pants role in the musical, a female playing a male.) Rosa's music teacher, Jasper, has composed **"Moonfall"** for her, and insists she sing it for him. The song's strange romantic longings reflect the dark mood of Dickens' novel. After Drood is killed, the audience votes on the identity of the murderer. If Rosa is chosen (unlikely) the invented plot is that she meant to kill Jasper in revenge for his lustful advances, but accidentally killed Drood because he was wearing Jasper's coat. The name of the musical was changed to *Drood* late in its Broadway run, but it is conventionally called by its original title.

## OKLAHOMA!
### Out of My Dreams

Music by Richard Rodgers
Lyrics and Book by Oscar Hammerstein II
Opened on Broadway 31 March 1943 for an initial run of 2212 performances

Based on the Lynn Riggs play *Green Grow the Lilacs*, *Oklahoma!* is a recognized landmark in the history of American musical theatre. Rodgers could not interest his longtime partner, Lorenz Hart, in the project, and began writing his first show with Hammerstein. A fusion of song, story, character, and dance created an example of a "book" show that was unified and dramatically sophisticated compared to most of the song and dance entertainments of the 1920s and 1930s. Agnes DeMille's choreography was a significant creative component. *Oklahoma!* is set in the summer of 1907 just prior to the Indian territory becoming Oklahoma and officially entering the United States. The musical spins a simple tale mostly concerned with whether the decent Curly or the menacing Jud gets to take Laurey to the box social. Though she chooses Jud in a fit of pique, Laurey really loves Curly. Singing **"Out of My Dreams,"** she unleashes her suppressed desires for Curly, as she watches in horror in a dream as the menacing Jud kills Curly. (The song appears briefly in the dream sequence at the end of Act I; Rodgers and Hammerstein wrote an extended version of the song, which appears in this edition.) Despite her feelings for Curly, Laurey fulfills her promise to attend the social with Jud. Things turn ugly when Laurey tells Jud she cannot return his feelings for her. He threatens her and she fires him as her farmhand. Laurey turns to Curly for comfort, and he proposes to her. At Laurey and Curly's wedding three weeks later they join in celebrating Oklahoma's impending statehood, then—after Jud is accidentally killed in a fight with Curly—the couple rides off in their surrey with the fringe on top. Before *Oklahoma!*, hit musicals generally ran one season on Broadway. *Oklahoma!* changed that pattern, establishing a new precedent for long-run musicals. *Oklahoma!* was among the first batch of new Broadway musicals to open in London after the end of World War II, playing there in 1947, achieving great success. The film version was released in 1955.

## 110 IN THE SHADE
### Old Maid

Music by Harvey Schmidt
Lyrics by Tom Jones
Book by N. Richard Nash
Opened on Broadway 24 October 1963 for an initial run of 330 performances

N. Richard Nash adapted his 1954 play, *The Rainmaker*, for Schmidt and Jones' first Broadway musical, following their wildly successful *The Fantasticks* Off-Broadway. (Nash's play is best remembered for the 1956 film version which starred Burt Lancaster and Katharine Hepburn.) The plot of the musical version remains quite faithful to that of the play. It is a simple tale of Lizzie, an unmarried woman who lives with her father and brothers on a drought-stricken ranch in the American southwest in July of 1936. Starbuck, a transient "rainmaker" comes on the scene and is soon seen to be the con man that he is, despite his dazzling charisma. He does, however, pay sincere attention to Lizzie, and awakens love and life in her. The song in this volume, **"Old Maid,"** is a moving aria that ends the first act, in which Lizzie nakedly reveals her fears of forever being alone. Though Starbuck dazzles her, she sees no future with him, and winds up with the more ordinary but reliable Sheriff File instead. A London production opened in 1967.

## PHANTOM
### This Place Is Mine

Music and Lyrics by Maury Yeston
Book by Arthur Kopit
Opened in Houston, 1991

At this writing Yeston's *Phantom* has not had a Broadway run, but has played on tour in the United States and has been widely produced. Based on the 1911 French novel by Gaston Leoux, the show's principal characters are Christine and the Phantom, who will not reveal his disfigured face. The Phantom dwells in the catacombs under the Paris opera house where Carlotta reigns as diva. He despises her, and teaches voice to Christine with the ambition of putting her on the stage instead. **"This Place Is Mine"** is Carlotta's comic song about the opera house she owns, where she jealously reigns. Yeston and Kopit actually wrote their show before Lloyd Webber wrote his, but were unable to get any financing for a Broadway production after the new British musical was announced.

## THE PHANTOM OF THE OPERA
### Think of Me
### Wishing You Were Somehow Here Again

Music by Andrew Lloyd Webber
Lyrics by Charles Hart and Richard Stilgoe
Book by Richard Stilgoe and Andrew Lloyd Webber
Opened 9 October 1986 in London
Opened on Broadway 26 January 1988

French novelist Gaston Leoux wrote *Le Fantôme de l'Opéra* after visiting the subterranean depths of the Paris Opera House, including its man-made lake. Though not a success when published in 1911, the ghoulish tale became internationally celebrated with the 1925 film starring Lon Chaney. Ken Hill's 1984 London stage production was seen by Lloyd Webber; after also reading the novel the composer of *Cats* decided that he would make *The Phantom of the Opera* his next musical. It is the story of a disfigured musical genius who haunts the trackless catacombs beneath the Paris Opera. The world's revulsion at his outer ugliness twists the artist within. He conceives a passion for a lovely young singer, Christine Daaé, and hypnotizes her into becoming his student and worshipper. Calling him the Angel of Music, she is willing to do anything for him. The Phantom's spell is broken with the arrival of a young man who vies with the Phantom for Christine's affections, Raoul. **"Think of Me"** is the aria the diva Carlotta sings in an opera in production. After an accident in rehearsal deliberately caused by the Phantom she storms off. The chorus girl Christine sings it for an audition, then in full operatic treatment on opening night as the new star. **"Wishing You Were Somehow Here Again"** is Christine's plea, after the Phantom's threat begins to grow, for the guidance of her dead father in how to balance the love of Raoul and her feelings of protection for the Phantom. Raoul plots to expose the Phantom and end the nightmare of his control, but the Phantom captures Christine. Raoul attempts to rescue her, but it is Christine's compassion to the Phantom that secures their release. When the mob arrives in his lair, the Phantom has escaped.

## RAGS

### Children of the Wind

Music by Charles Strouse
Lyrics by Stephen Schwartz
Book by Joseph Stein
Opened on Broadway 21 August 1986 for an initial run of 4 performances

On paper, *Rags* looked like a sure hit, with music by Charles Strouse, lyrics by Stephen Schwartz, and starring charismatic opera star Teresa Stratas. However, this sprawling musical, set in 1910 in New York's Lower East Side, and chronicling the lives of the Jewish immigrants who made their way there, could not find favor in its short Broadway run. The score features a wide range of music, including Klezmer, Ragtime, and musical comedy. Rebecca Hershkowitz (Teresa Stratas in the original cast) arrives with her young son at Ellis Island hoping to find her husband, who left Russia for America years before and has not communicated with her since. Feeling displaced and lonely soon after arrival, in **"Children of the Wind"** Rebecca likens the rootless disintegration of her family, and similar situations for all refugees, to being tossed about by the elements. She gets a job as a seamstress in a sweatshop, falls in love with union organizer Saul, reunites with her husband Nathan, who she finds disturbingly disconnected to their Jewish heritage, but eventually starts a new life with Saul. The show was later revised.

## SHE LOVES ME

### Will He Like Me?
### Dear Friend
### Vanilla Ice Cream

Music by Jerry Bock
Lyrics by Sheldon Harnick
Book by Joe Masteroff
Opened on Broadway 23 April 1963 for an initial run of 301 performances

The closely integrated, melody drenched score of *She Loves Me* is certainly one of the best ever written for a musical comedy. Set in the 1930s in Budapest, the tale is of the people who work in Maraczek's Parfumerie, principally the constantly squabbling sales clerk Amalia Balash and the manager Georg Nowack. It is soon revealed that they are anonymous romantic pen pals who agree to meet one night at the Café Imperiale, though neither knows the other's identity. Amalia worries about the upcoming first date in **"Will He Like Me?"** Georg sees that it is Amalia who is waiting for him in the restaurant, but doesn't let on. He attempts to engage her, but they argue and she sends him away, leaving her to sit there waiting in vain, culminating in **"Dear Friend."** After she calls in sick the next day their relationship blossoms into love when Georg visits her, plants some worry in her mind about the man of the letters whom she believes she has never met, and brings her ice cream. After he leaves she realizes how wrong she was about Georg in **"Vanilla Ice Cream."** Eventually, Georg is emboldened to reveal his identity by quoting from one of Amalia's letters. Amalia would have been played by Julie Andrews had she not been filming *Mary Poppins*. Amalia Balash in *She Loves Me* turned out to be one of Barbara Cook's most magical portrayals. A London West End production opened in 1964. *Parfumerie*, the Hungarian play by Miklós László on which *She Loves Me* is based, had been used as the basis for two films, *The Shop Around the Corner* (1940) and *In the Good Old Summertime* (1949). Yet another film, *You've Got Mail* (1998), was loosely adapted from the same story.

## SHOW BOAT

### Make Believe
### Can't Help Lovin' Dat Man
### Bill

Music by Jerome Kern
Lyrics and Book by Oscar Hammerstein II
Opened on Broadway 27 December 1927 for an initial run of 572 performances

No show ever to hit Broadway was more historically important, and at the same time more beloved than *Show Boat*, that landmark of the 1927 season. (Any musical that ran more than one year, held over into the next season, was an enormous success in this period.) Edna

Ferber's popular 1926 novel of life on the Mississippi was the source for this musical/operetta, and provided a rich plot and characters which Kern and Hammerstein amplified to become some of the most memorable ever to grace the stage. *Show Boat* was a mixture of the American operetta style, based on British and Viennese models, and the new American musical theatre style, and presented a rare example of complete congruity which would later blossom in the more adventurous book musicals of the 1930s, '40s and '50s. Captain Andy Hawks heads a traveling troop of players on his show boat, the *Cotton Blossom*, that ambles up and down the river towns of the Mississippi. Soon after docking at Natchez, Mississippi, Andy's daughter Magnolia meets a riverboat gambler, Gaylord Ravenal. He mistakenly thinks that Magnolia is an actress; she is not (yet), but is happy to **"Make Believe"** with him. The duet has been adapted as a solo for this edition. Magnolia excitedly tells her actress friend Julie about the dashing man she has just met. Julie cautions her that he may be a worthless drifter, and says it's not easy to stop loving a man, illustrated in **"Can't Help Lovin' Dat Man."** (In the context of the show this song is presented as an old favorite in an upbeat minstrel style, not in the slow and dreamy style of the 1951 film version.) In the famous miscegenation scene the local sheriff charges that Julie is a mulatto, born of a black mother, and by the laws of the day against mixed marriages, was illegally married to a white man, Steve. Knowing the sheriff is coming Steve pricks Julie's finger and sucks the blood, telling the sheriff that he has black blood in him. The sheriff agrees to let them go after all have backed them up, but Julie and Steve leave, as black performers are not allowed on show boats in 1887. Magnolia is heartbroken, but buoyed by Captain Andy asking Ravenal to play the romantic lead in the play. Against her mother's wishes, Magnolia becomes an actress. She and Ravenal marry. The couple moves to Chicago eventually, and end up in poverty due to Ravenal's gambling. He leaves his wife and child, ashamed. It is now 1893. Magnolia gets a job singing at a Chicago nightclub on New Year's Eve, the same nightclub where Julie, now an alcoholic on the skids after Steve left her, has just been rehearsing **"Bill."** Without Magnolia's knowledge Julie sacrificially bows out of the show, making room for her friend. More than 30 years pass. Magnolia has become a star of stage and radio, as has her daughter, Kim. Magnolia returns to the *Cotton Blossom* and meets Ravenal for the first time in decades. The couple reunites as Joe sings a reprise of "Ol' Man River."

*Show Boat* played in London in 1928. Modern productions have often transposed the soprano role of Julie down into a theatre belter range. The 1936 film version of *Show Boat* is most close to the original Broadway production. The 1951 film version made significant changes to the musical. Particularly for a classical singer, it will likely be instructive to hear the excellent 1988 studio recording of *Show Boat*, with Frederica von Stade as Magnolia, Teresa Stratas as Julie, and Jerry Hadley as Ravenal. This recording included all the material cut from the score during its 1927 Broadway try-out tour.

## 1600 PENNSYLVANIA AVENUE

### Take Care of This House

Music by Leonard Bernstein
Lyrics and Book by Alan Jay Lerner
Opened on Broadway 4 May 1976 for an initial run of 7 performances

The address of the title is of the White House. The musical focuses on the building and its inhabitants, including presidents, first ladies, staff and servants, assaults on the White House in its early years, as well as exploring class and racial issues through the eyes of servants. From Act I, **"Take Care of This House,"** the stand-out ballad from the score, was sung by first lady Abigail Adams as the term of her husband ends and Thomas Jefferson's presidency begins. *1600 Pennsylvania Avenue* was Leonard Bernstein's last Broadway musical. Although it was not a success, and he withdrew the work from his canon, he remained fond of the score and used some of its themes in later works. A one-hour concert version, *A White House Cantata*, was created after Bernstein's death.

## THE SOUND OF MUSIC

### The Sound of Music
### Climb Ev'ry Mountain

Music by Richard Rodgers
Lyrics by Oscar Hammerstein II
Book by Howard Linsay and Russel Crouse
Opened on Broadway 16 November 1959 for an initial run of 1443 performances

Set in Austria in 1938 before and during the Anschluss (the Nazi annexing of Austria to Germany), *The Sound of Music* is based on the book *The Trapp Family Singers* by Maria Augusta Trapp. As the show opens, Maria Rainer sings **"The Sound of Music"** admiring the Alps outside of the abbey where she lives. She gives evidence of her free spirit, appreciation of nature, and her love of music before she is reminded of her neglected duties. Following her Mother Abbess's instructions to go into the world to confirm her convictions about intending to take vows to become a nun, Maria reluctantly agrees to leave the abbey to serve as governess to the widower Captain von Trapp's seven children. After bonding with the children and bringing music back into the previously glum household, Maria becomes afraid of the new feelings she has for the engaged-to-be-married Captain von Trapp. She returns to the abbey. The wise Mother Abbess offers Maria encouragement in deciding to face Captain von Trapp, singing **"Climb Ev'ry Mountain."** As millions who have seen the film know, she returns to marry the Captain, and the family escapes Salzburg as the Nazis take control. *The Sound of Music* was the final Rodgers and Hammerstein collaboration. Hammerstein wrote both book and lyrics for all their musicals together except *The Sound of Music*, for which he wrote lyrics only. He was ill during the writing and died of stomach cancer on 23 August 1960, months after the show's Broadway opening. The London run, opening in 1961, far surpassed the Broadway run in number of performances. Though a success on Broadway and London, the popularity of the musical skyrocketed following the release of the 1965 film version, for which Rodgers contributed additional songs. Maria's songs were originally in a lower key for the voice of Mary Martin for the stage musical, but were transposed up to a soprano range for Julie Andrews for the film.

## SPRING IS HERE

### With a Song in My Heart

Music by Richard Rodgers
Lyrics by Lorenz Hart
Book by Owen Davis
Opened on Broadway 11 March 1929 for an initial run of 104 performances

Owen Davis adapted his play, *Shotgun Wedding*, for the musical *Spring Is Here*. Terry loves Betty, who thinks she loves Stacy. In an early scene in Act I Betty and Stacy sing the romantic **"With a Song in My Heart,"** each singing a verse in a convention of the time. The song has something of the operetta style still being heard on Broadway in the 1920s. Betty and Stacy are about to elope, but her father stops them. Terry flirts with other girls to get Betty's attention. It works. Betty realizes she loves Terry, and the happy ending has them coming together. Musical comedies of this period had slim plots and were light in style. The lasting aspects for many shows of the 1920s and 1930s were not their totality as book musicals, but the shining moments of great songs such as this one.

## STREET SCENE

### What Good Would the Moon Be?

Music by Kurt Weill
Lyrics by Langston Hughes
Book by Elmer Rice
Opened on Broadway 9 January 1947 for an initial run of 148 performances

Kurt Weill persuaded Elmer Rice to write the libretto based on his own Pulitzer Prize-winning 1929 play, with poet Langston Hughes supplying the imaginative lyrics. Billed as "a dramatic musical," the blending of drama and music was very close to opera. In fact, *Street Scene* has found productions most often by opera companies. In Act I, Rose reluctantly agrees to allow her boss, the married Harry Easter, to walk her home after they go out dancing after work. He tries to seduce her in his song "Wouldn't You Like to Be on Broadway?" Rose, who is about 19 and living with her parents, replies that her wishes are simpler and romantic, and clearly not about Harry, in **"What Good Would the Moon Be?"** *Street Scene* loosely frames a series of vignettes with a large cast of characters, depicting a slice of life in hot summer in the lower east side New York tenement setting. The story deals principally with the brief, star-crossed romance of Sam Kaplan and Rose Maurrant, and the tragic consequences of the infidelity of Rose's mother when her husband shoots her and her lover. *Street Scene* is an expansive example of Weill's belief that Broadway was the only place to develop a new style of American opera.

## SWEENEY TODD

### Green Finch and Linnet Bird

Music and Lyrics by Stephen Sondheim
Book by Hugh Wheeler
Opened on Broadway 1 March 1979 for an initial run of 557 performances

In 19th century London Benjamin Barker, who now calls himself Sweeney Todd, has returned after escaping imprisonment in Australia on a trumped-up charge cooked up by Judge Turpin, who desired Barker's wife, Lucy. Johanna, Barker's teenage daughter, is the ward of Judge Turpin and confined to his house, recognizing her kinship with the caged birds in **"Green Finch and Linnet Bird."** Anthony, a young sailor, falls in love with her after seeing her in her window, and attempts to help her escape the Judge's intentions of marrying her. Angered by Johanna's rebuff of him the Judge commits Johanna to an insane asylum. Anthony rescues her, and in the process all the lunatics break free. In the principal plot Todd and Mrs. Lovett, who owns a meat pie shop, concoct a scheme to murder barber clients and use their carcasses for pie filling. Todd's motive is to get the Judge in the chair to enact revenge on him. Todd kills the Judge, among many others. Todd recognizes an insane beggar woman as his wife Lucy and kills Mrs. Lovett for her duplicity in telling him that Lucy was dead. Tobias, a simple boy who has been working for Mrs. Lovett cuts Todd's throat. *Sweeney Todd* opened in London in 1980.

The fictional story of Sweeney Todd first appeared in "The String of Pearls: A Romance," with no author credit, in the British magazine *The People's Periodical and Family Library*, in 18 weekly installments, 1846–47. It was immediately adapted as a play and opened in London in 1847. The story was lengthened and expanded into a 732 page novel and published in London in 1850 as *The String of Pearls*, with the subtitle *The Barber of Fleet Street: A Domestic Romance*. The 1865 play adaptation remained popular for decades in Britain. The story was again adapted for the stage in 1973 by British playwright Christopher Bond, which was the basis for the musical *Sweeney Todd*. Non-musical film versions of the story were released in 1926, 1928, 1936, 1970, and for television in 1973, 1998 and 2006. A film version of the musical was released in 2007.

## SWEET ADELINE

### Why Was I Born?

Music by Jerome Kern
Lyrics and Book by Oscar Hammerstein II
Opened on Broadway 3 September 1929 for an initial run of 234 performances

*Sweet Adeline* was intended as a vehicle for Helen Morgan, the original Julie in *Show Boat*, also by Kern and Hammerstein. Set in and around New York in 1898, the story concerns Addie Schmidt, the daughter of a Hoboken beer garden owner, and her three loves. After Tom Martin has gone to fight in the Spanish-American war, Addie, now known as Adeline Belmont, becomes a Broadway star and falls for wealthy socialite James Day. But his family disapproves and she happily ends up in the arms of composer Sid Barnett. The show capitalized on the brief nostalgia for the 1890s around the year 1930. *Sweet Adeline* was more an operetta in style, a late example of the genre on Broadway, than modern musical. Down on her luck and blue after a break-up, a lovesick Adeline melodramatically ponders **"Why Was I Born?,"** a great torch song. A movie version starring Irene Dunne was released in 1935.

## TWO BY TWO

### The Golden Ram

Music by Richard Rodgers
Lyrics by Martin Charnin
Book by Peter Stone
Opened on Broadway 10 November 1970 for an initial run of 343 performances

After an absence of almost thirty years, Danny Kaye returned to Broadway in a musical based on the biblical story of Noah and the Ark. Adapted from Clifford Odets' play, *The Flowering Peach*, *Two by Two* deals primarily with the ancient Noah's rejuvenation and his relationship with his wife and family as he undertakes the formidable task of building the ark and gathering all creatures in pairs, commanded by God. Noah and Esther's three sons and their wives are the human passengers on the ark. Japheth's fun-loving wife, Goldie, finds herself a better match for Ham, and Japheth finds he's a better match with Ham's wife, Rachel. In a coloratura seduction scene Goldie sings **"The Golden Ram"** to Ham. Madeline Kahn played Goldie in the original cast.

## WEST SIDE STORY

### I Feel Pretty
### Somewhere

Music by Leonard Bernstein
Lyrics by Stephen Sondheim
Book by Arthur Laurents
Opened on Broadway 26 September 1957 for an initial run of 732 performances

*West Side Story* is loosely based on William Shakespeare's *Romeo and Juliet*. Gangs rule the streets of the west side of New York City in the 1950s, before the area was revitalized with the construction of Lincoln Center in the 1960s. The Jets are tough Americans, in hate-filled rivalry with the Sharks, tough Puerto Ricans. Tony, a former Jet trying to go straight with a regular job, meets Maria, sister to one of the Sharks, at a dance held at a gym. They instantly fall in love, drawing anger from Maria's brother, Bernardo, leader of the Sharks. Riff, leader of the Jets, challenges the Sharks to a rumble. Tony later secretly visits Maria's fire escape balcony, where they confirm their love, uniting as one the next day, after business hours, in the bridal shop where Maria works. That evening Tony goes to the rumble to try to stop it, but when Bernardo stabs Riff, Tony instinctively stabs and kills Bernardo. As this is happening, before she knows of Bernardo's death, in her bedroom Maria confesses to her friends her emotions at being in love in **"I Feel Pretty,"** which opens Act II. Maria learns from Chino, a Shark, that Tony has killed Bernardo just before Tony steals into her bedroom. First enraged and bitter, she settles down in Tony's embrace, and they dream of a safe and peaceful place away from the gang-ridden existence in the city. After a ballet representing this dream a character simply called A Girl sings **"Somewhere."** Chino later shoots and kills Tony, and Maria grieves over his body. A London production opened in 1958 and surpassed the number of Broadway performances. The 1961 film version retained most of the score, but made significant shifts in song and scene order.

## WICKED

### Let Us Be Glad

Music and Lyrics by Stephen Schwartz
Book by Winnie Holzman
Opened on Broadway 30 October 2003

The musical was based on the 1995 novel *Wicked: The Life and Times of the Wicked Witch of the West* by Gregory Maguire. The story speculates on the back story of the Wicked Witch of the West, Elphaba, and Good Witch of the North, Glinda (Galinda), before their story threads are picked up in L. Frank Baum's *The Wonderful Wizard of Oz*. As the musical begins, the citizens of Oz celebrate the death of the Wicked Witch of the West, led by Glinda singing **"Let Us Be Glad."** A flashback begins that tells the story of the complex relationship between the misunderstood Elphaba Thropp and the ambitious Galinda Upland. Glinda and Elphaba form a friendship in secret and unite against the duplicitous Wizard. Fiyero winds up with Elphaba, whose staged death at being melted is a hoax.

# FALLING IN LOVE WITH LOVE
### from *The Boys from Syracuse*

Words by Lorenz Hart
Music by Richard Rodgers

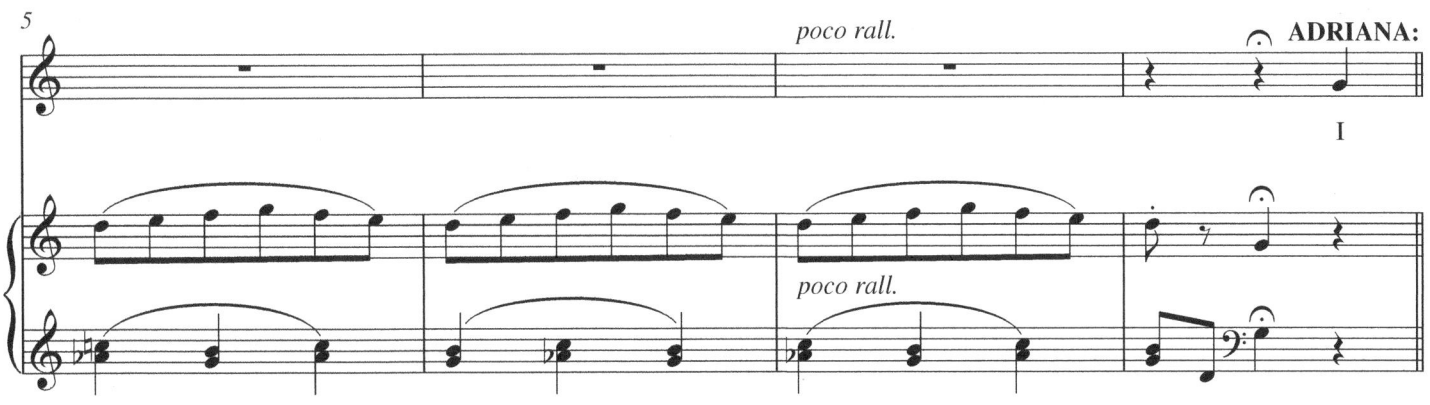

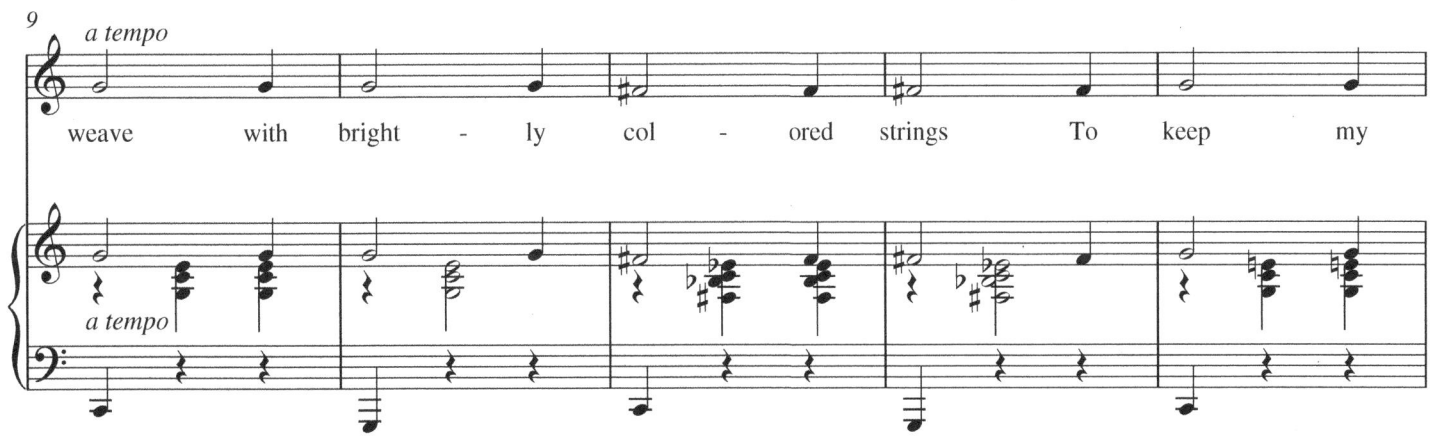

Copyright © 1938 (Renewed) by Chappell & Co.
Rights for the Extended Renewal Term in the U.S. Controlled by Williamson Music and WB Music Corp. o/b/o The Estate Of Lorenz Hart
International Copyright Secured   All Rights Reserved

19
fin - gers dance.
24
And keep your hands out of ro - mance.
29
Love - ly
33
witch - es Let the stitch - es Keep your fin - gers

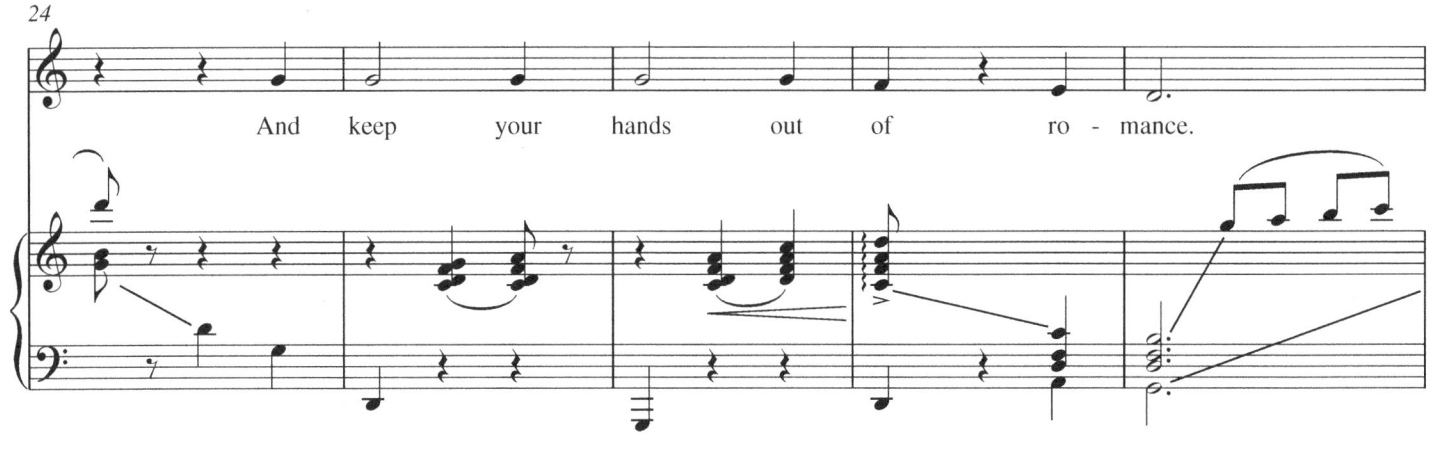

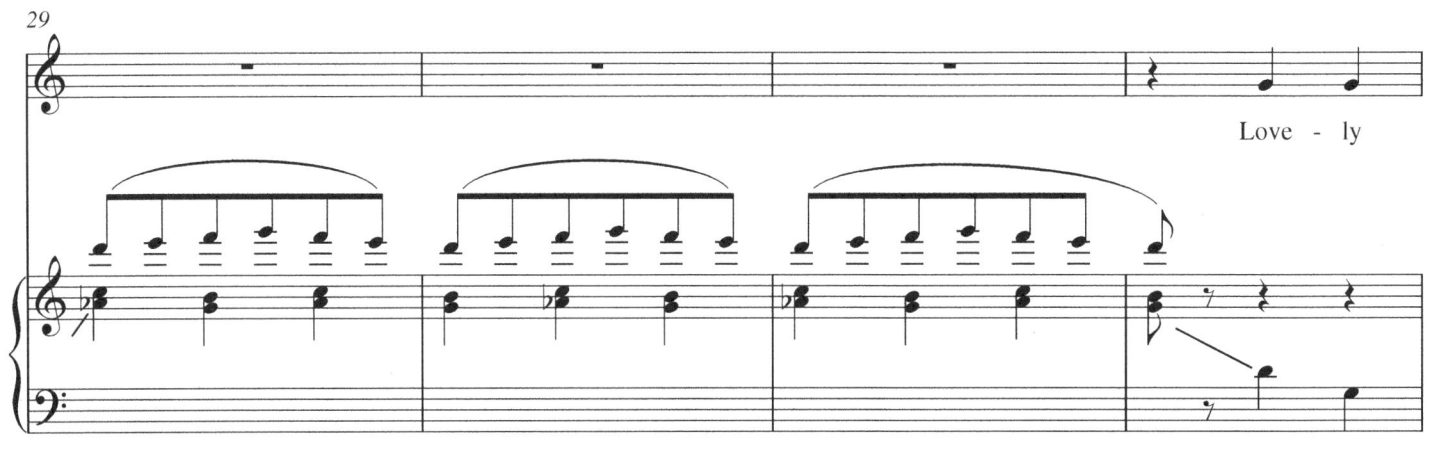

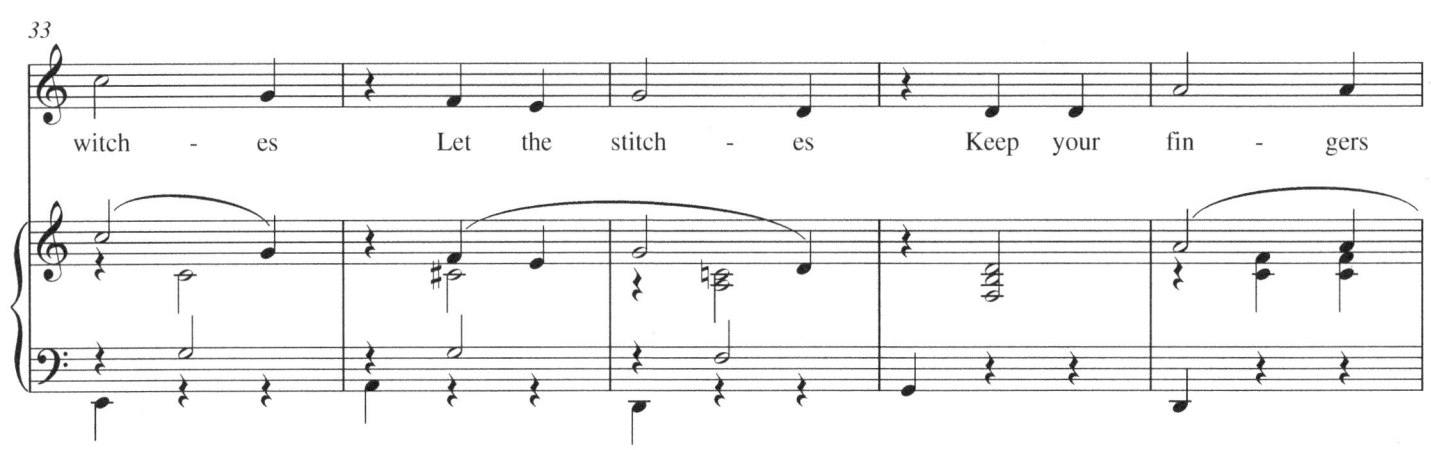

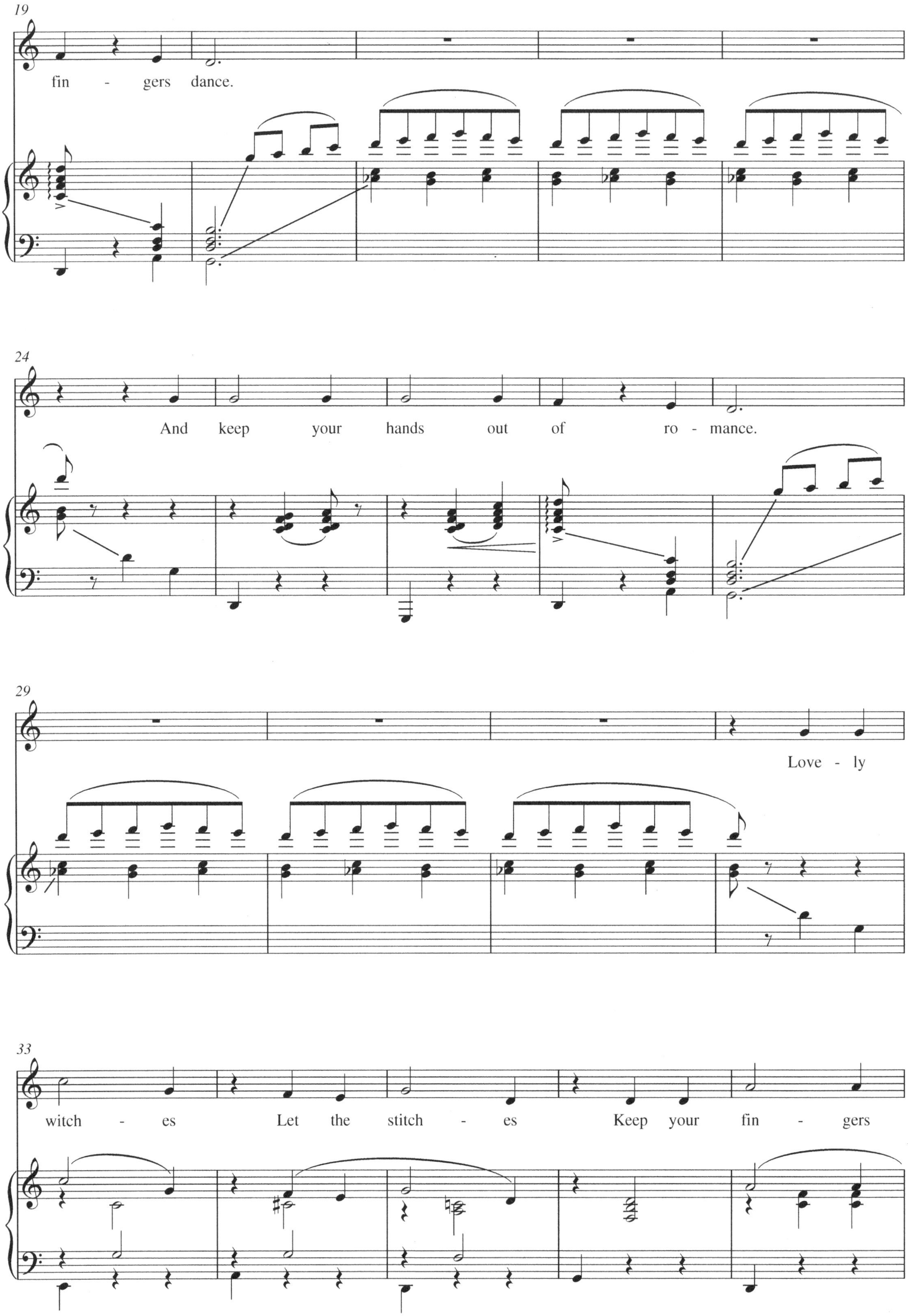

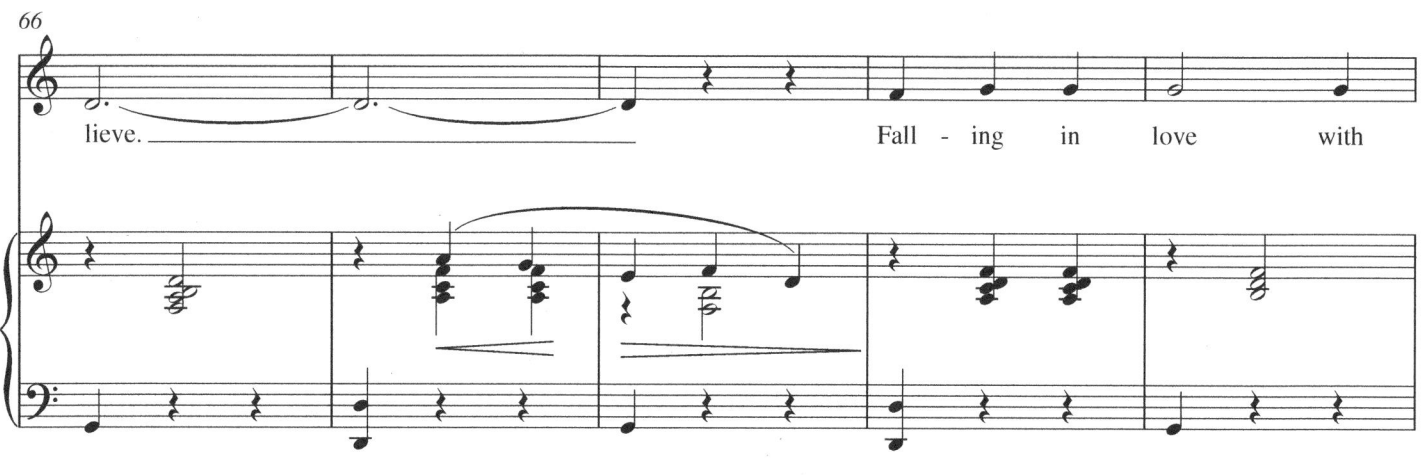

96
night when the moon was full.
101
I was un - wise with eyes Un - a - ble to see.
cresc. poco a poco
106
I fell in love with
111
rall.
love, With love ev - er - last - ing,
rall.

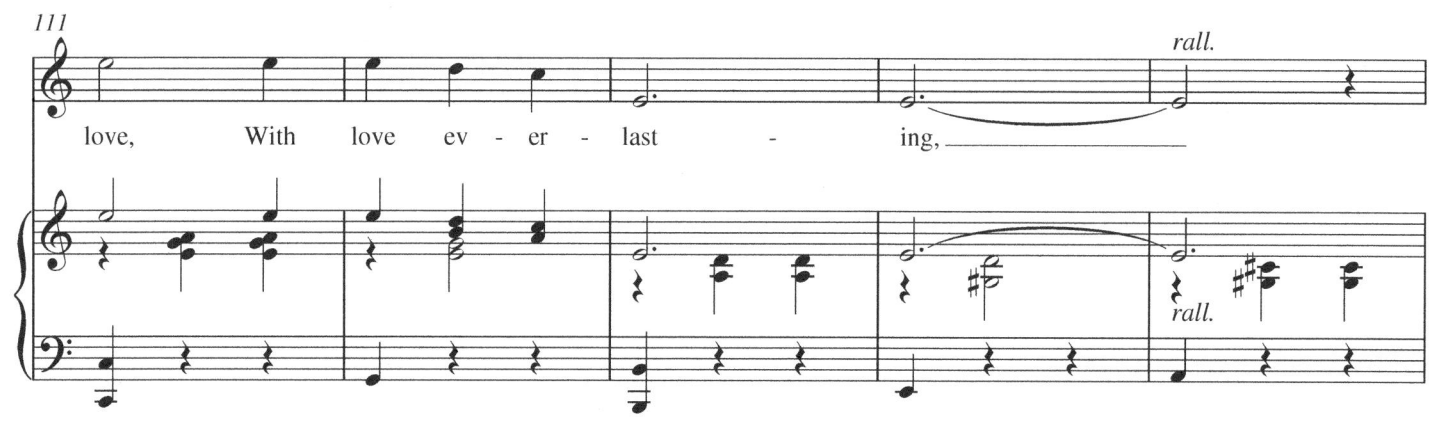

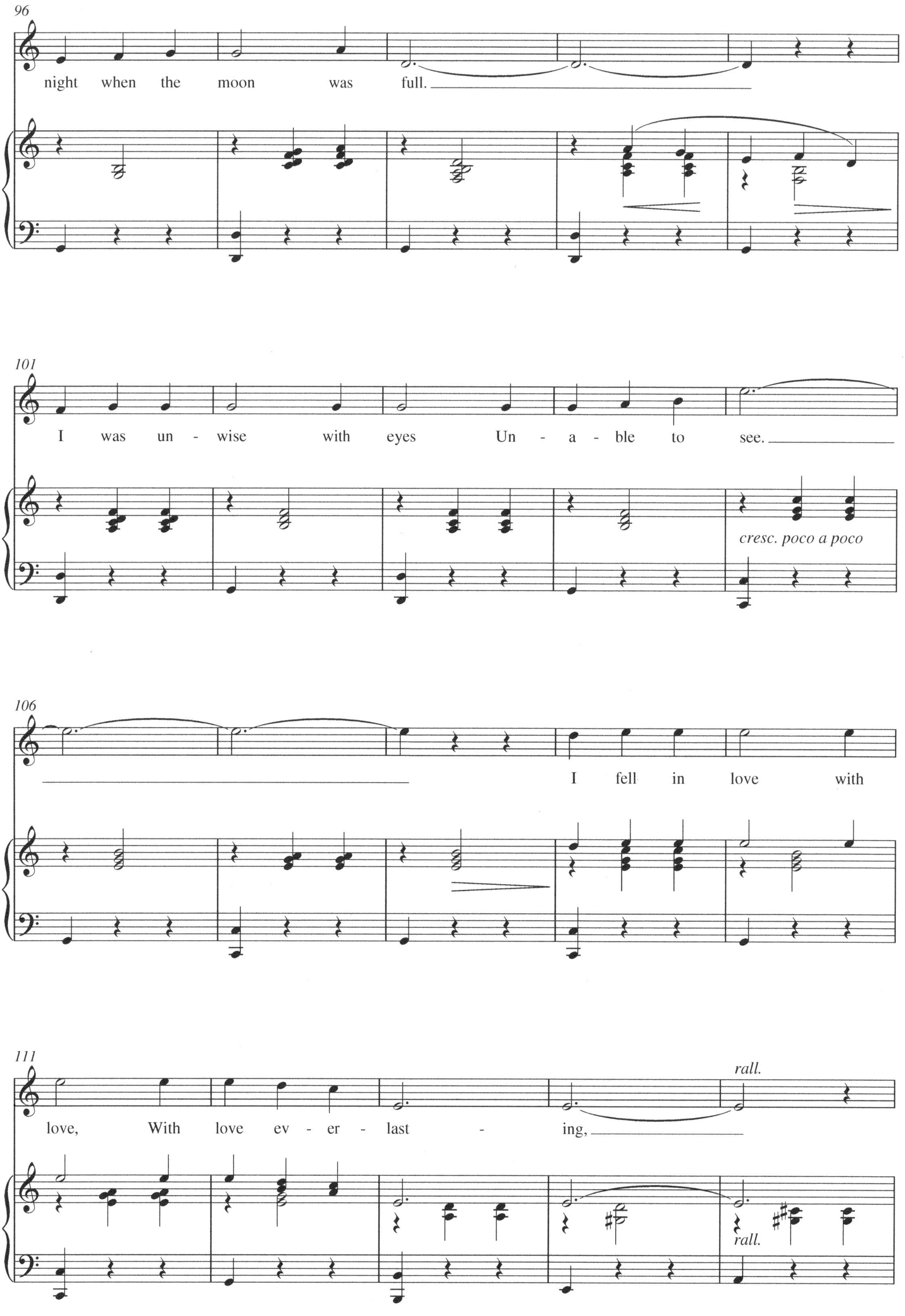

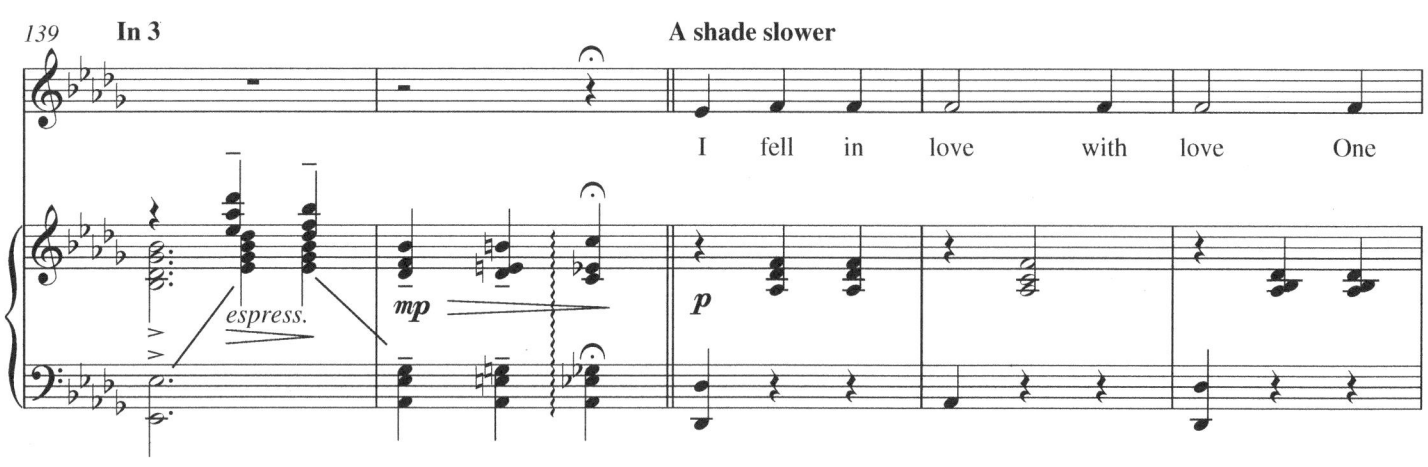
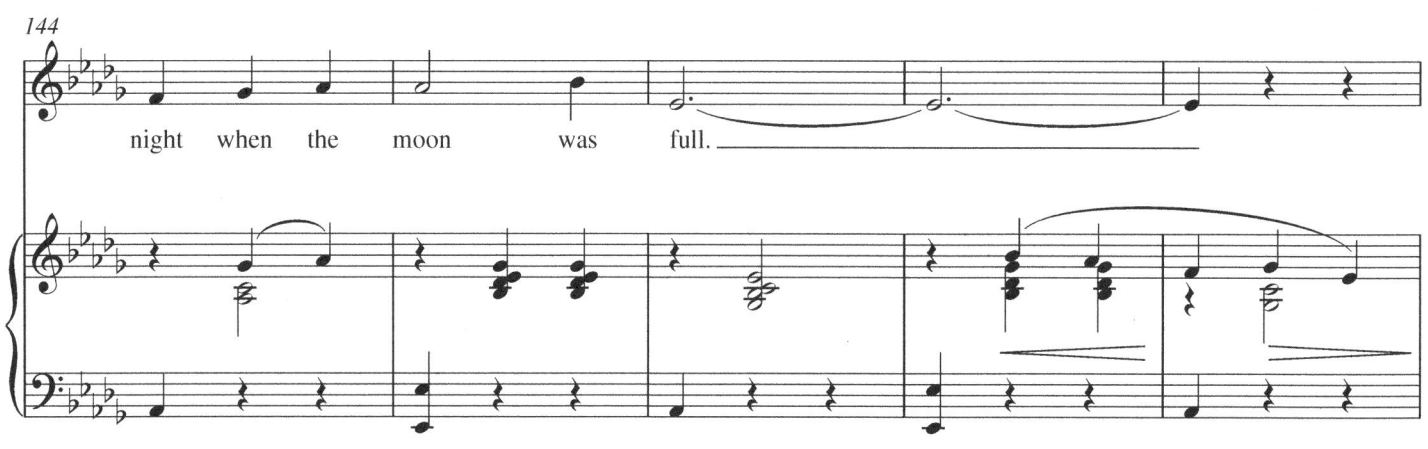

# MISTER SNOW
from *Carousel*

Lyrics by Oscar Hammerstein II
Music by Richard Rodgers

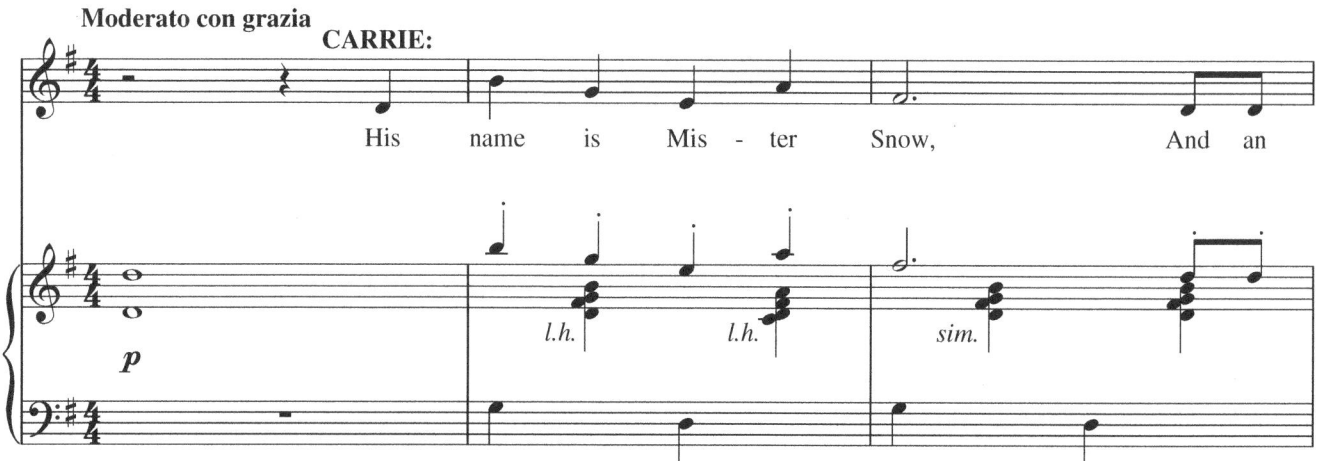

Copyright © 1945 by WILLIAMSON MUSIC
Copyright Renewed
International Copyright Secured  All Rights Reserved

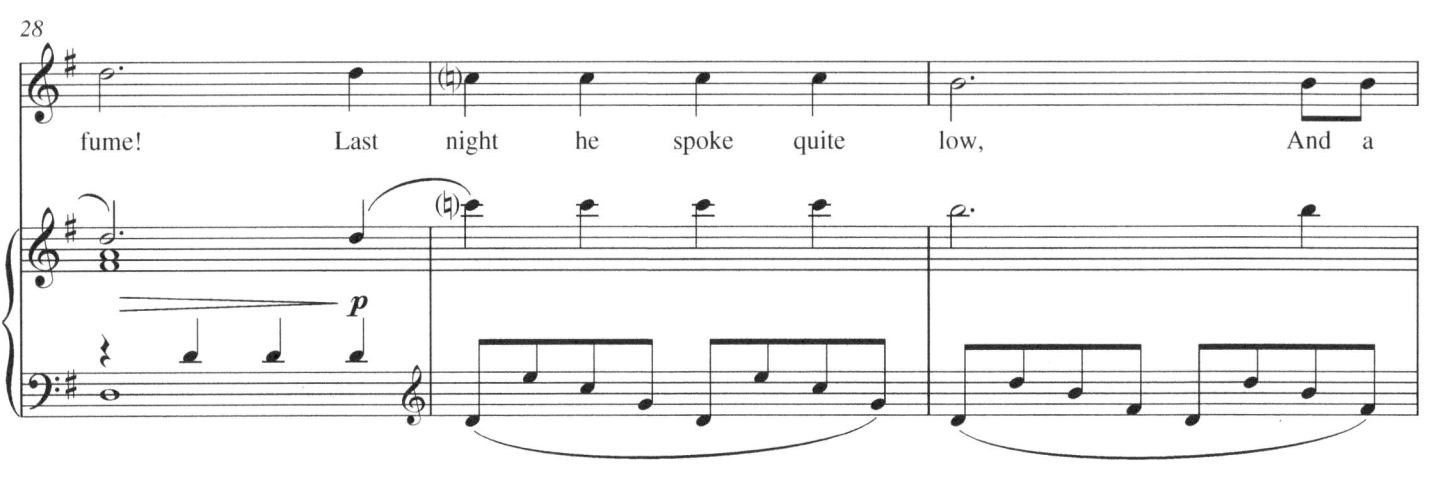

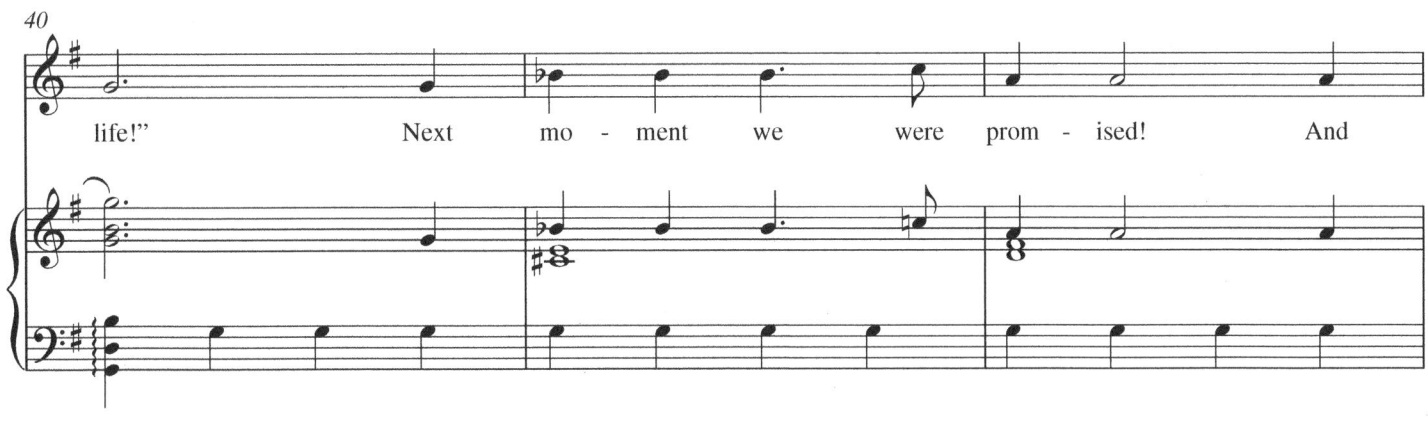

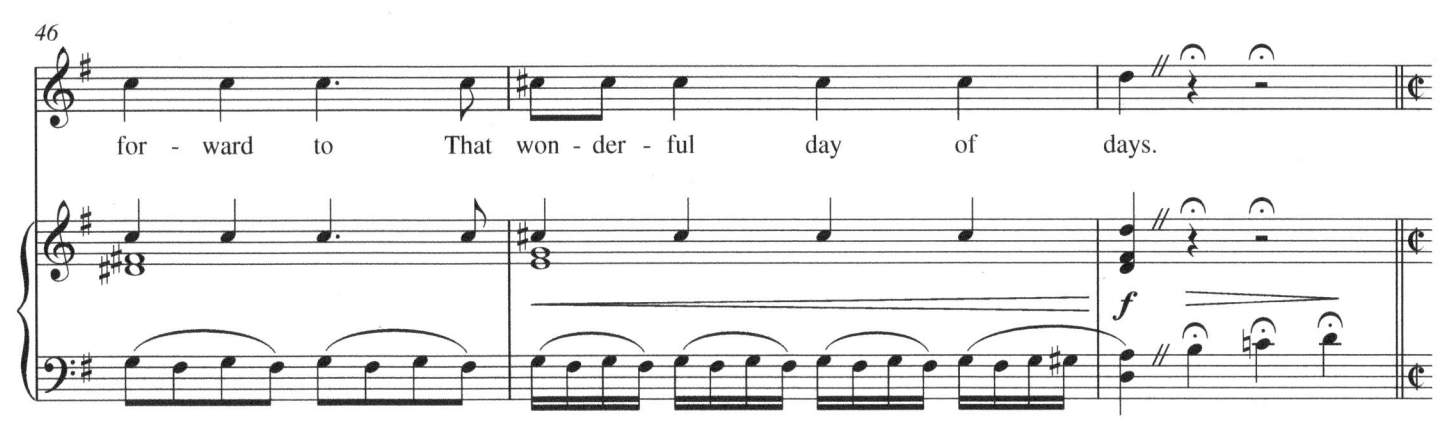

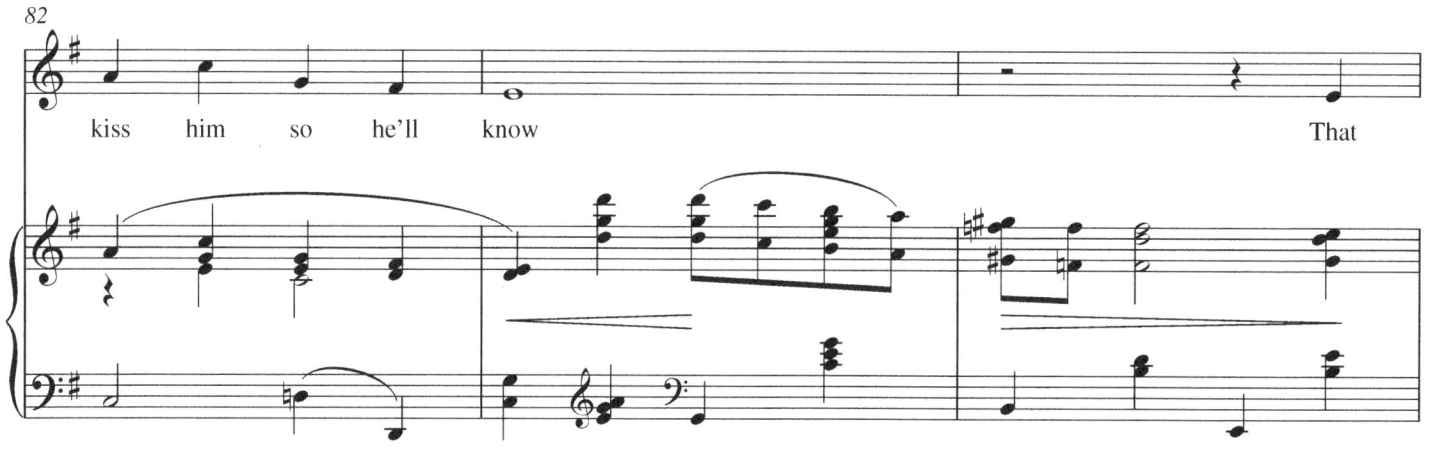

# IF I LOVED YOU
## from *Carousel*

Lyrics by Oscar Hammerstein II
Music by Richard Rodgers

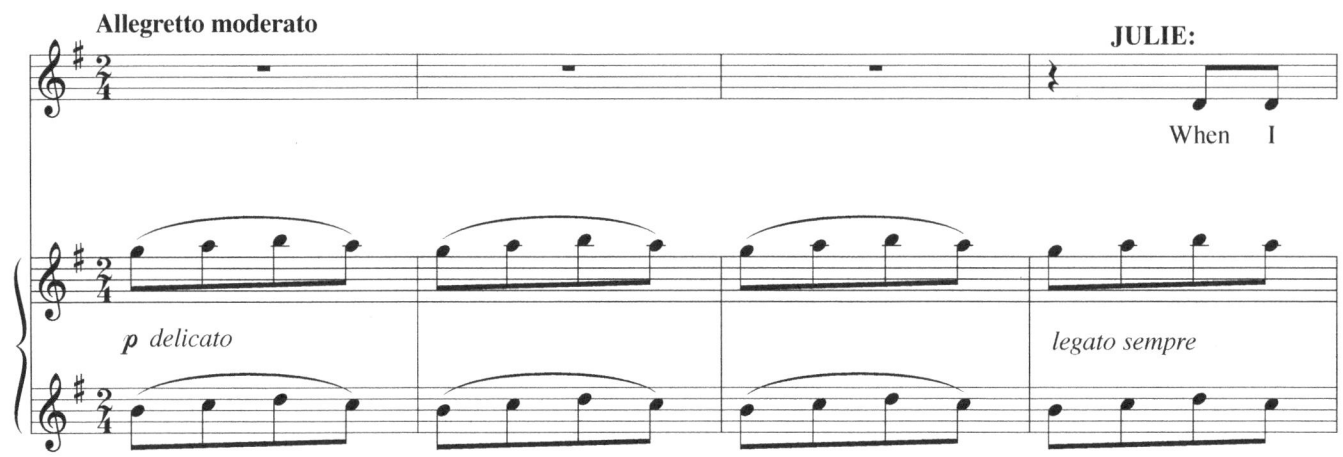

Copyright © 1945 by WILLIAMSON MUSIC
Copyright Renewed
International Copyright Secured   All Rights Reserved

# WHAT'S THE USE OF WOND'RIN'
from *Carousel*

Lyrics by Oscar Hammerstein II
Music by Richard Rodgers

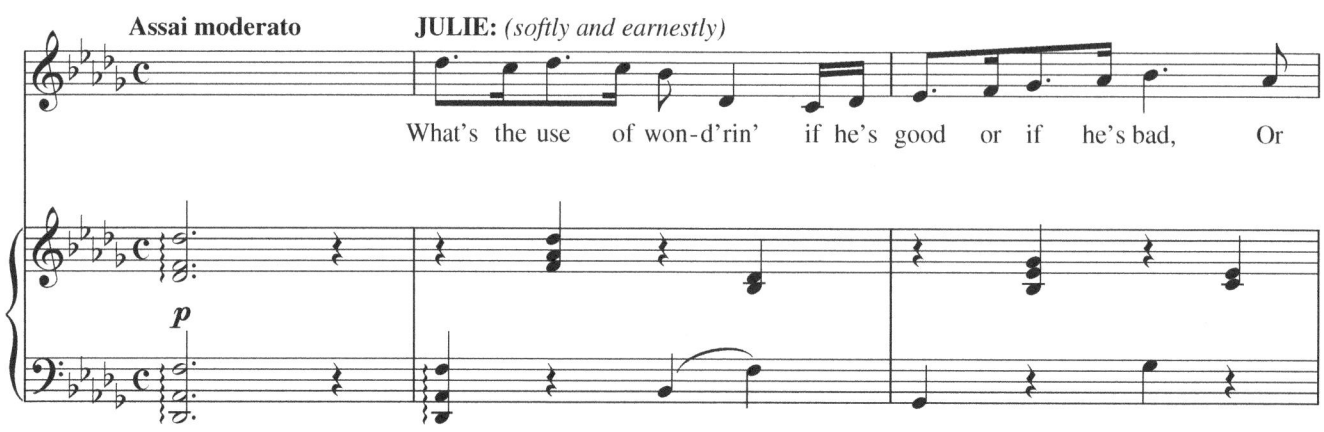

Copyright © 1945 by WILLIAMSON MUSIC
Copyright Renewed
International Copyright Secured   All Rights Reserved

# YOU'LL NEVER WALK ALONE
from *Carousel*

Lyrics by Oscar Hammerstein II
Music by Richard Rodgers

# ART IS CALLING FOR ME

from *The Enchantress*

Music by Victor Herbert
Lyrics by Harry B. Smith

\* treechy
\*\* optional lyric: "Songbirds" replacing "plump girls"

# I HAVE TO TELL YOU
## from *Fanny*

Words and Music by
Harold Rome

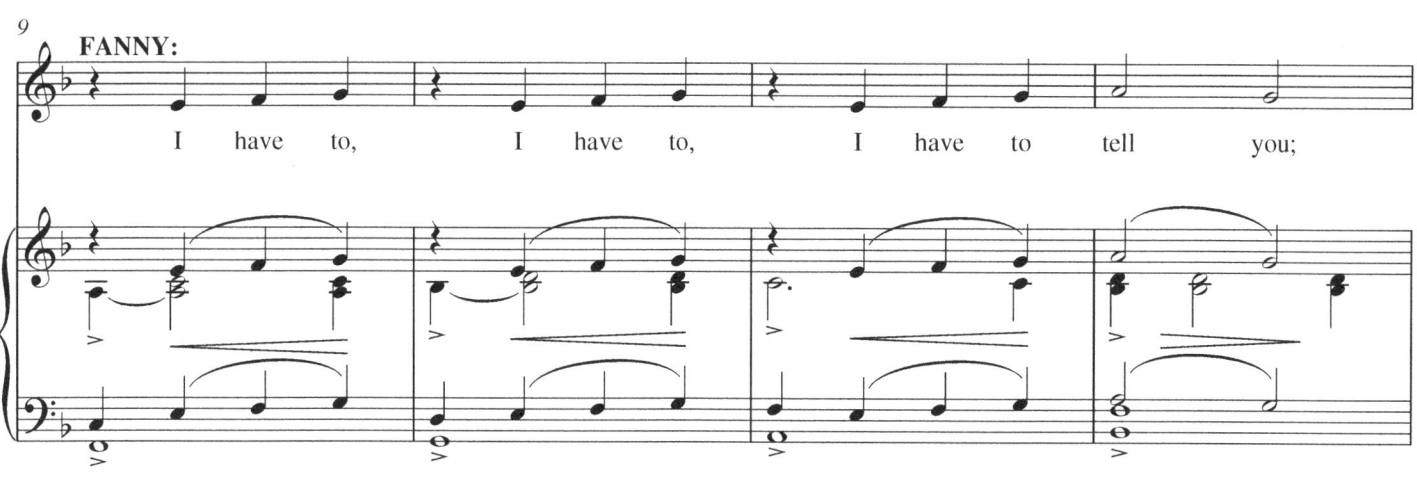

Copyright © 1954 by Harold Rome
Copyright Renewed
International Copyright Secured   All Rights Reserved

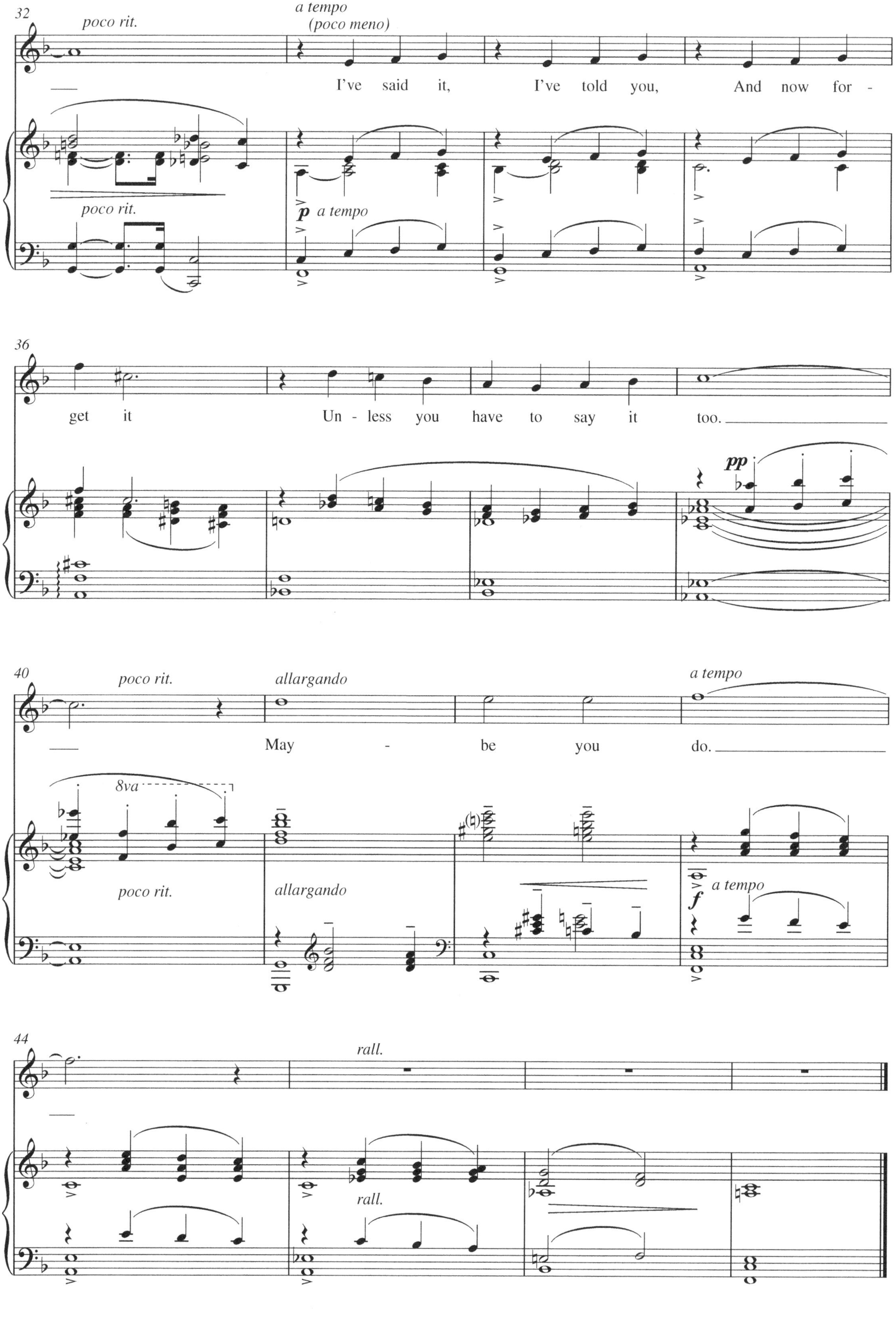
32
poco rit.
a tempo
(poco meno)
I've said it, I've told you, And now for -
poco rit.
p a tempo
36
get it Un - less you have to say it too.
pp
40
poco rit.
allargando
a tempo
May - be you do.
8va
poco rit.
allargando
f a tempo
44
rall.
rall.

# WHEN DID I FALL IN LOVE
from the Musical *Fiorello!*

Words by Sheldon Harnick
Music by Jerry Bock

Copyright © 1959 Bock IP LLC and Mayerling Productions, Ltd. in the U.S.A.
Copyright Renewed 1987
All Rights for Mayerling Productions, Ltd. Administered by R&H Music
All Rights for the world excluding the U.S.A. Administered by Alley Music Corp. and Bug Music-Trio Music Company
International Copyright Secured   All Rights Reserved

*Alternate beginning; voice would enter in measure 27.

# LOVE, LOOK AWAY
from *Flower Drum Song*

Lyrics by Oscar Hammerstein II
Music by Richard Rodgers

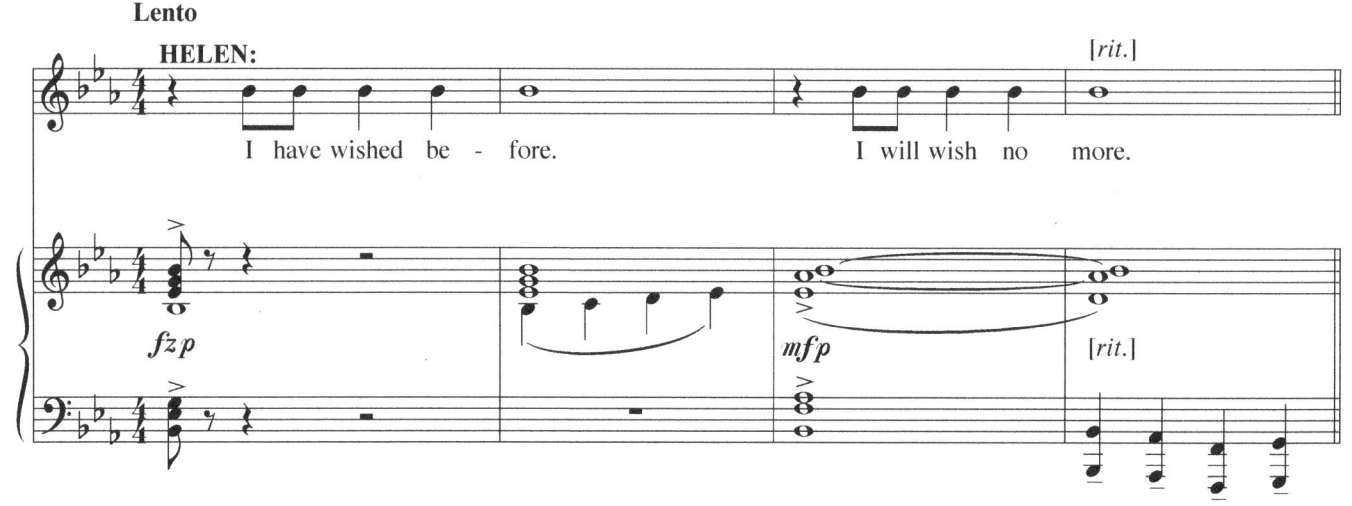

Copyright © 1958 by Richard Rodgers and Oscar Hammerstein II
Copyright Renewed
WILLIAMSON MUSIC owner of publication and allied rights throughout the world
International Copyright Secured   All Rights Reserved

# WILL YOU?
## from *Grey Gardens*

Music by Scott Frankel
Lyrics by Michael Korie

**EDITH:** *Good afternoon everyone, and welcome to Grey Gardens. I'd like to commence our little tribute to young love with one of our all-time favorites. Gould?—"Will You?"*

When li-lacs re-turn in spring, will you? When

*If the dialogue is omitted at the beginning, the song may be started at the Cantabile tempo. "Gould" is a reference to a musician.*

Copyright © 2006, 2007 by Staunch Music and Korie Music
Publishing and Allied Rights Administered by Williamson Music throughout the world
International Copyright Secured   All Rights Reserved

* If the dialogue is omitted, a possible cut may be made from * to **.

# ONE MORE KISS
from *Follies*

Music and Lyrics by
Stephen Sondheim

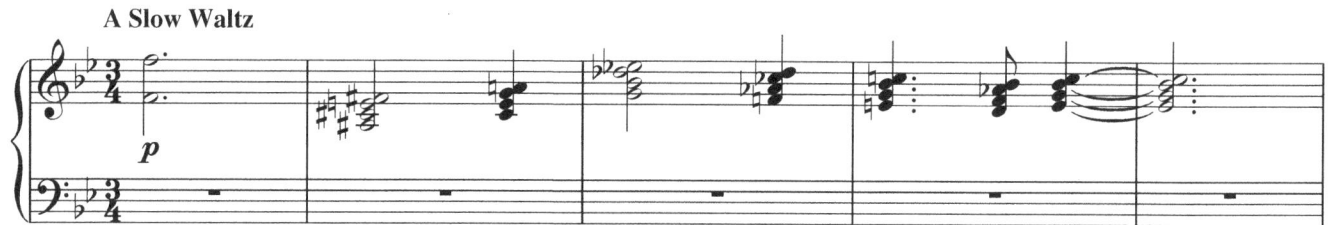
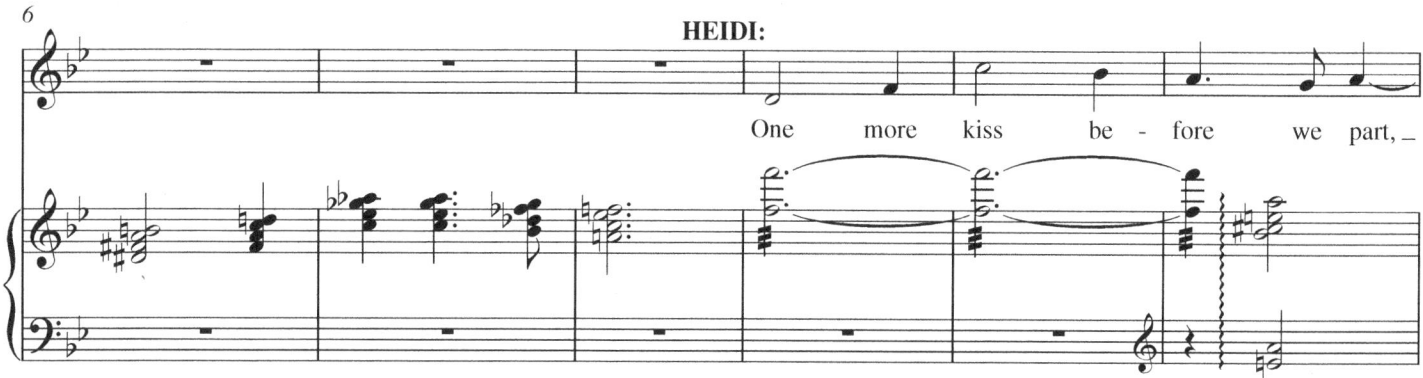

*In the show this song is sung as a duet (two sopranos).*

Copyright © 1971 by Range Road Music Inc., Jerry Leiber Music, Mike Stoller Music, Rilting Music, Inc. and Burthen Music Co., Inc.
Copyright Renewed
All Rights Administered by Herald Square Music, Inc.
International Copyright Secured   All Rights Reserved
Used by Permission

*The optional notes, an editorial addition, are a possibility to consider.*

54

# MY LORD AND MASTER
## from *The King and I*

Lyrics by Oscar Hammerstein II
Music by Richard Rodgers

Copyright © 1951 by Richard Rodgers and Oscar Hammerstein II
Copyright Renewed
WILLIAMSON MUSIC owner of publication and allied rights throughout the world
International Copyright Secured   All Rights Reserved

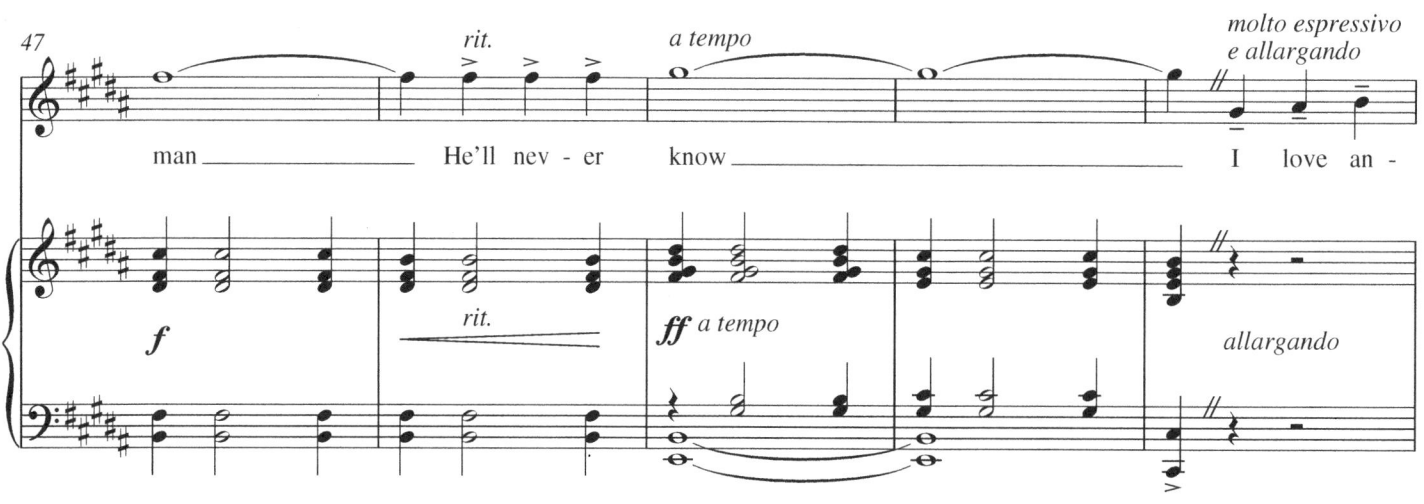
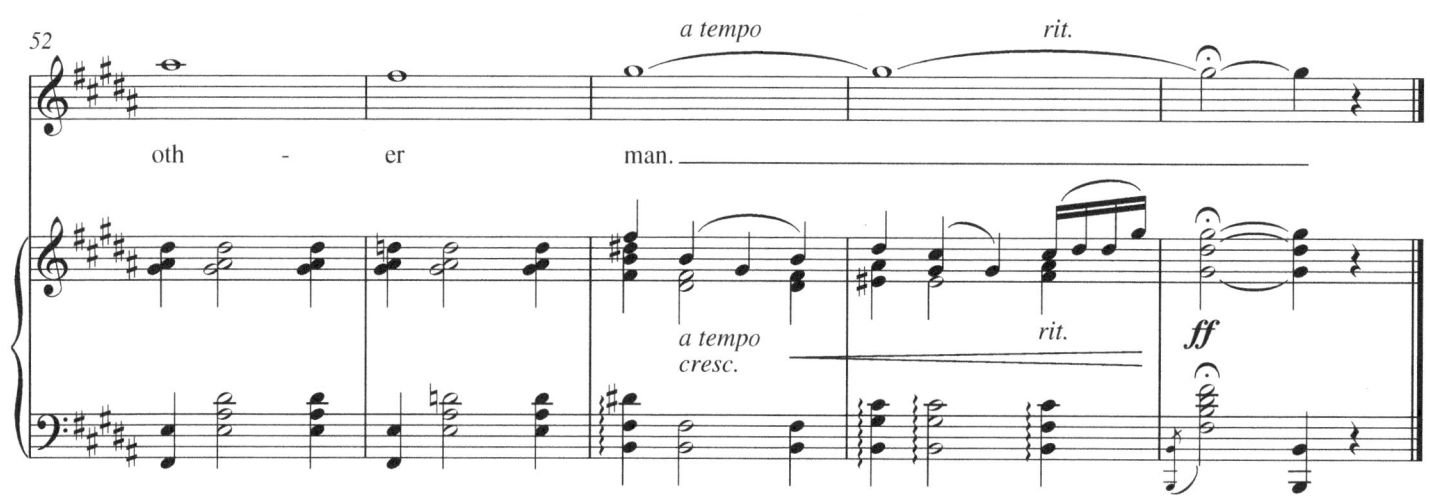

# HELLO, YOUNG LOVERS
from *The King and I*

Lyrics by Oscar Hammerstein II
Music by Richard Rodgers

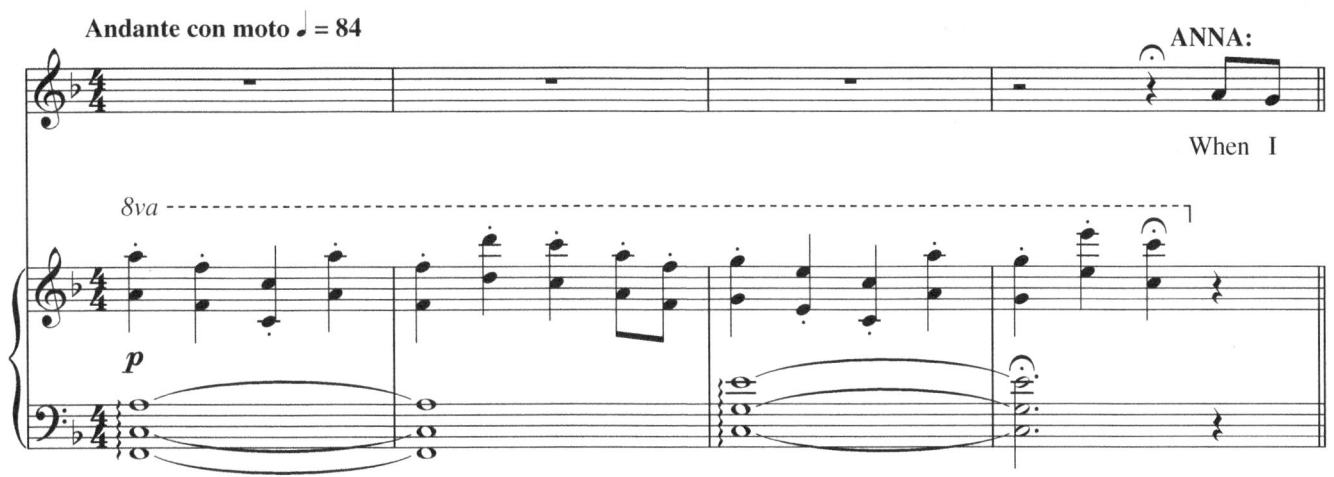

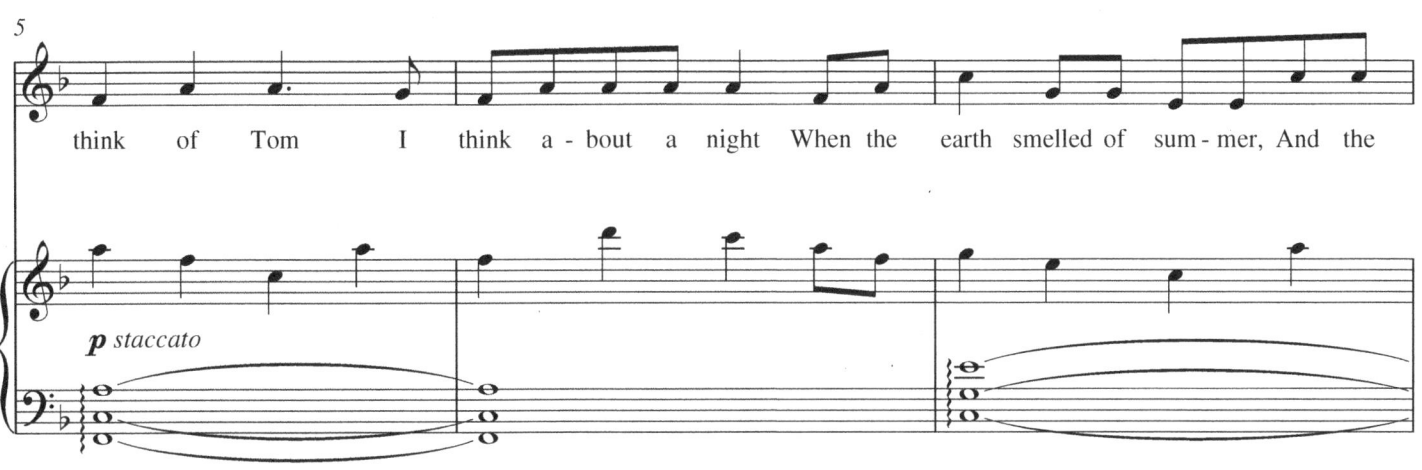

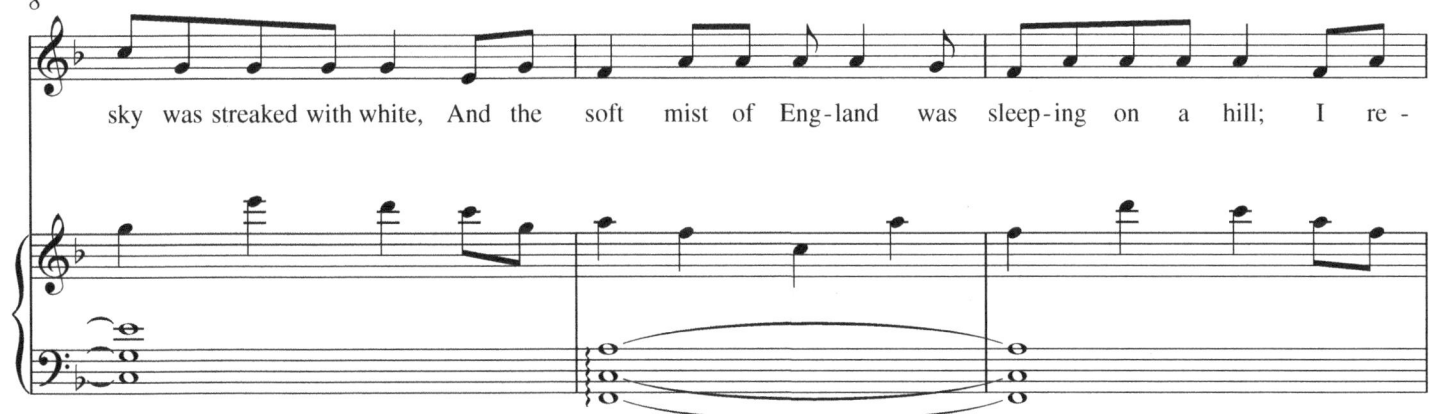

*Transposed up for this edition. Original key: D Major.*

Copyright © 1951 by Richard Rodgers and Oscar Hammerstein II
Copyright Renewed
WILLIAMSON MUSIC owner of publication and allied rights throughout the world
International Copyright Secured   All Rights Reserved

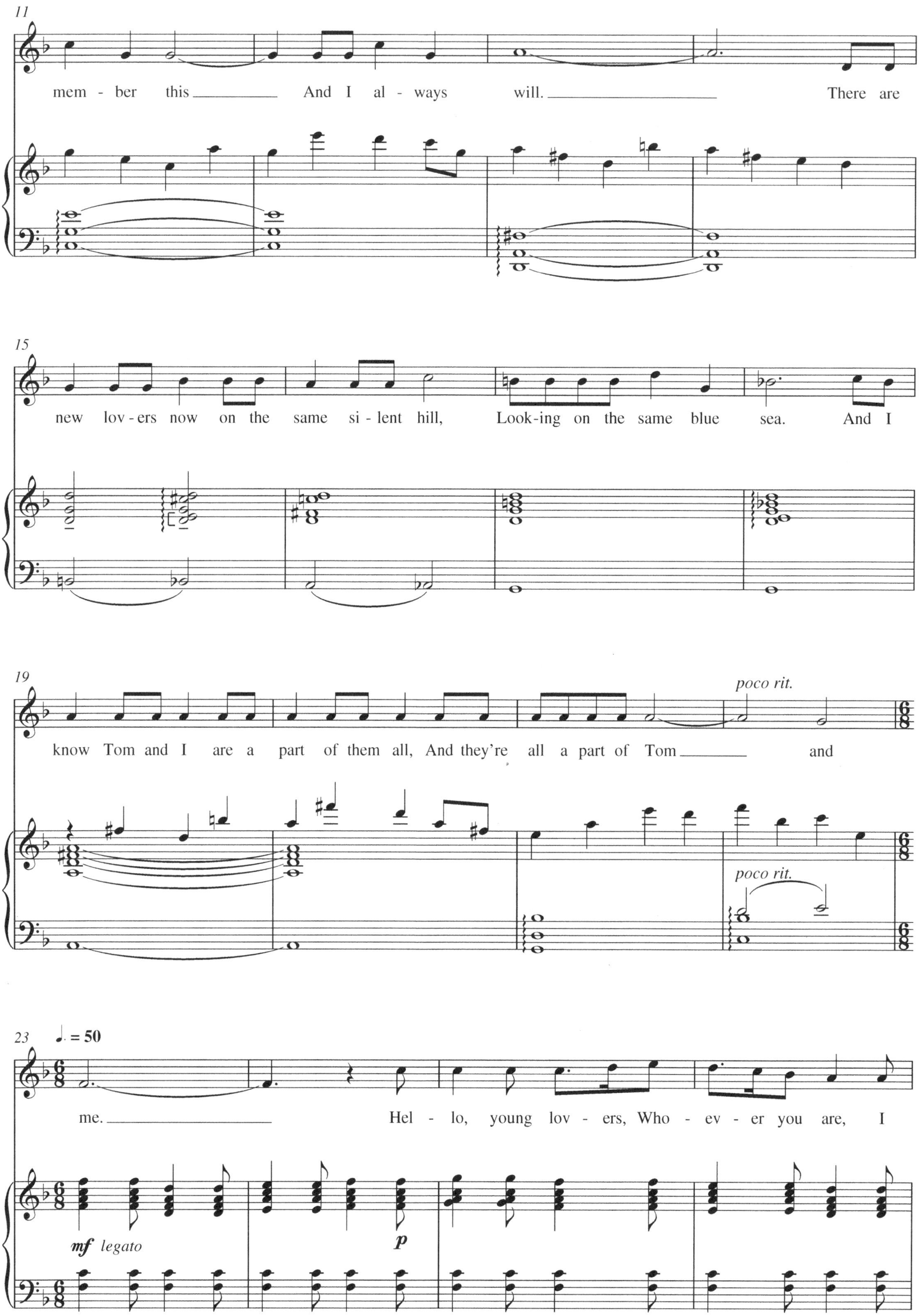
11
mem - ber this And I al - ways will. There are
15
new lov - ers now on the same si - lent hill, Look-ing on the same blue sea. And I
19
poco rit.
know Tom and I are a part of them all, And they're all a part of Tom and
poco rit.
23
♩. = 50
me. Hel - lo, young lov - ers, Who - ev - er you are, I
mf legato
p

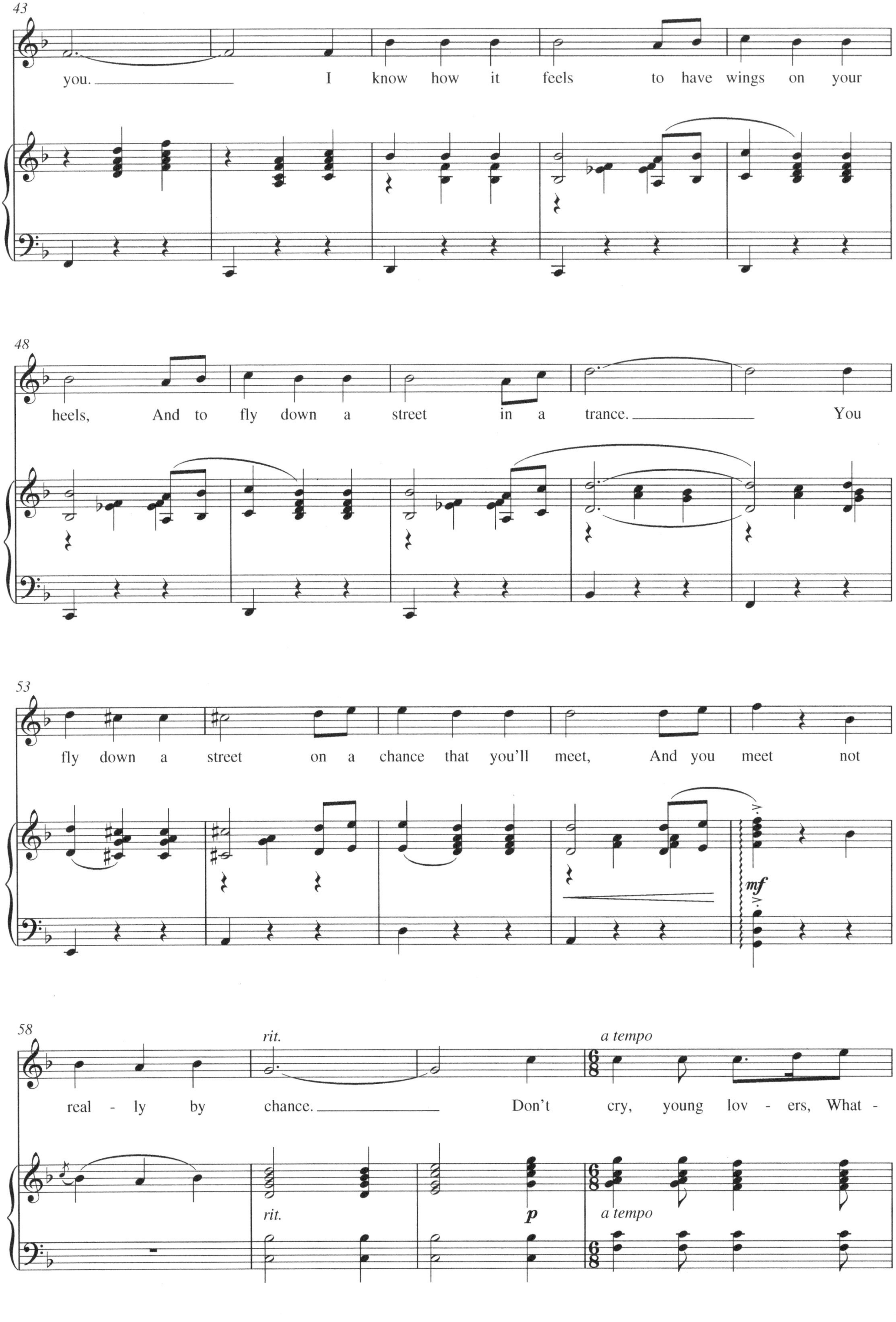
43
you. I know how it feels to have wings on your
48
heels, And to fly down a street in a trance. You
53
fly down a street on a chance that you'll meet, And you meet not
mf
58
rit.
a tempo
real - ly by chance. Don't cry, young lov - ers, What -
rit.
p
a tempo

62

# WE KISS IN A SHADOW
from *The King and I*

Lyrics by Oscar Hammerstein II
Music by Richard Rodgers

*This song is a duet for Lun Tha and Tuptim, adapted as a solo for this edition.*

Copyright © 1951 by Richard Rodgers and Oscar Hammerstein II
Copyright Renewed
WILLIAMSON MUSIC owner of publication and allied rights throughout the world
International Copyright Secured   All Rights Reserved

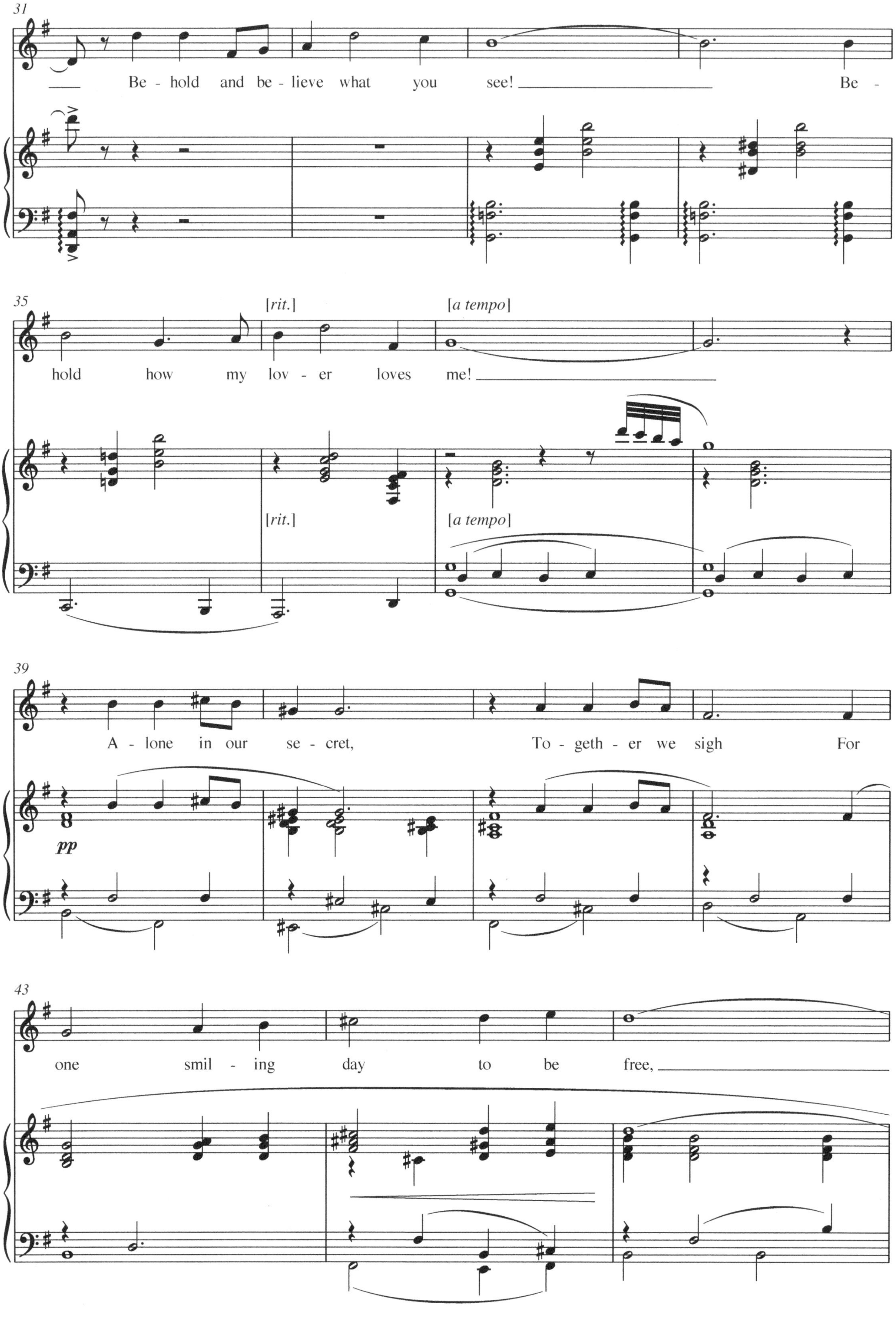
31
Be - hold and be - lieve what you see! Be -
35
[rit.]
[a tempo]
hold how my lov - er loves me!
[rit.]
[a tempo]
39
A - lone in our se - cret, To - geth - er we sigh For
pp
43
one smil - ing day to be free,

# I HAVE DREAMED
## from *The King and I*

Lyrics by Oscar Hammerstein II
Music by Richard Rodgers

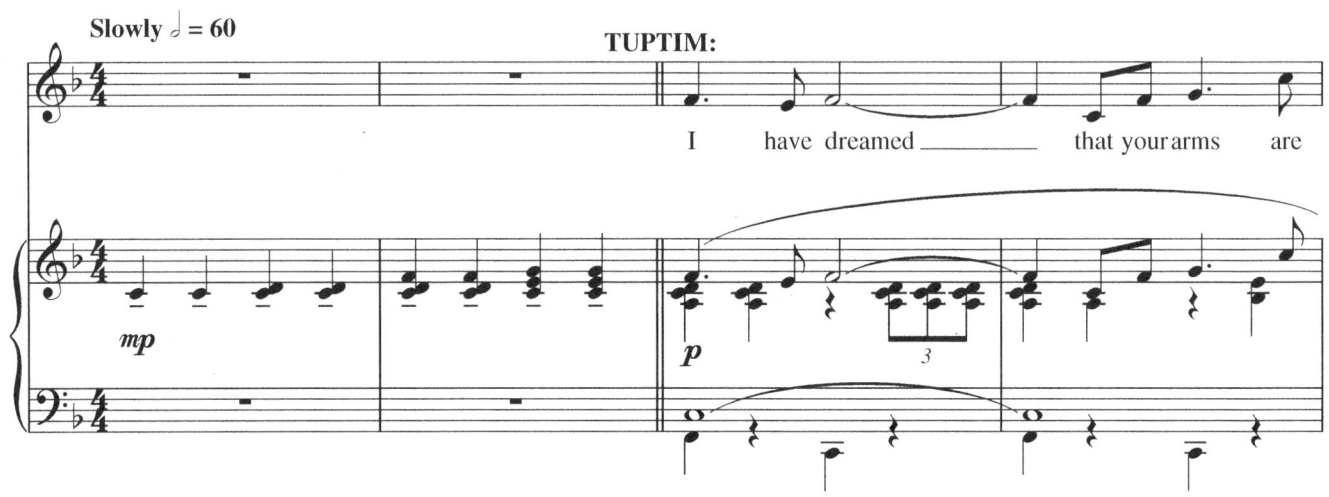

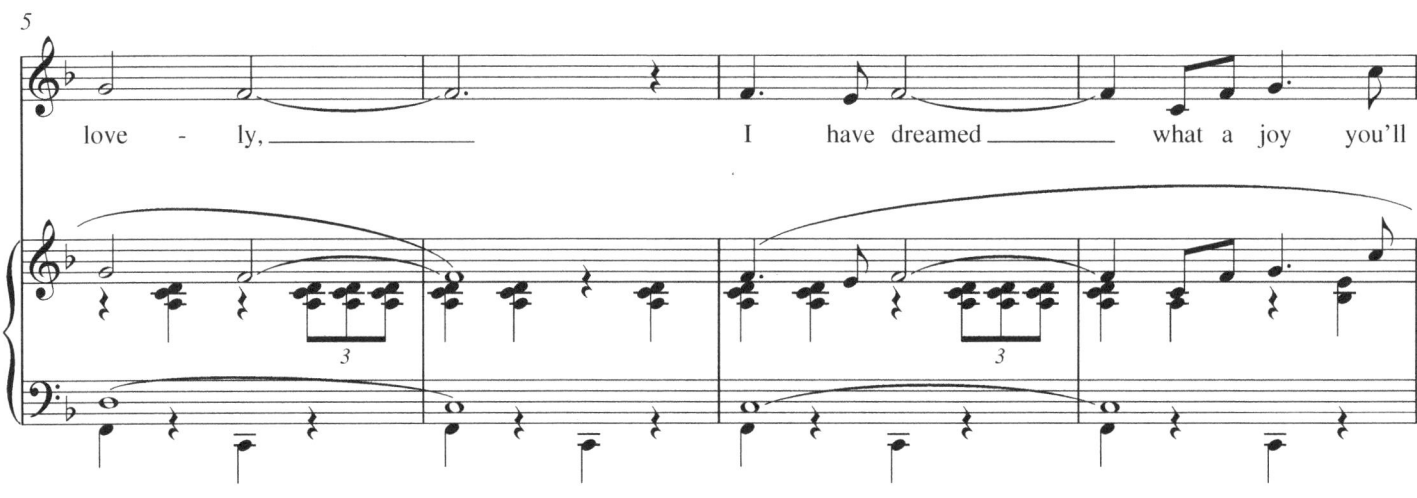

*This duet has been adapted as a solo for this edition.*

Copyright © 1951 by Richard Rodgers and Oscar Hammerstein II
Copyright Renewed
WILLIAMSON MUSIC owner of publication and allied rights throughout the world
International Copyright Secured   All Rights Reserved

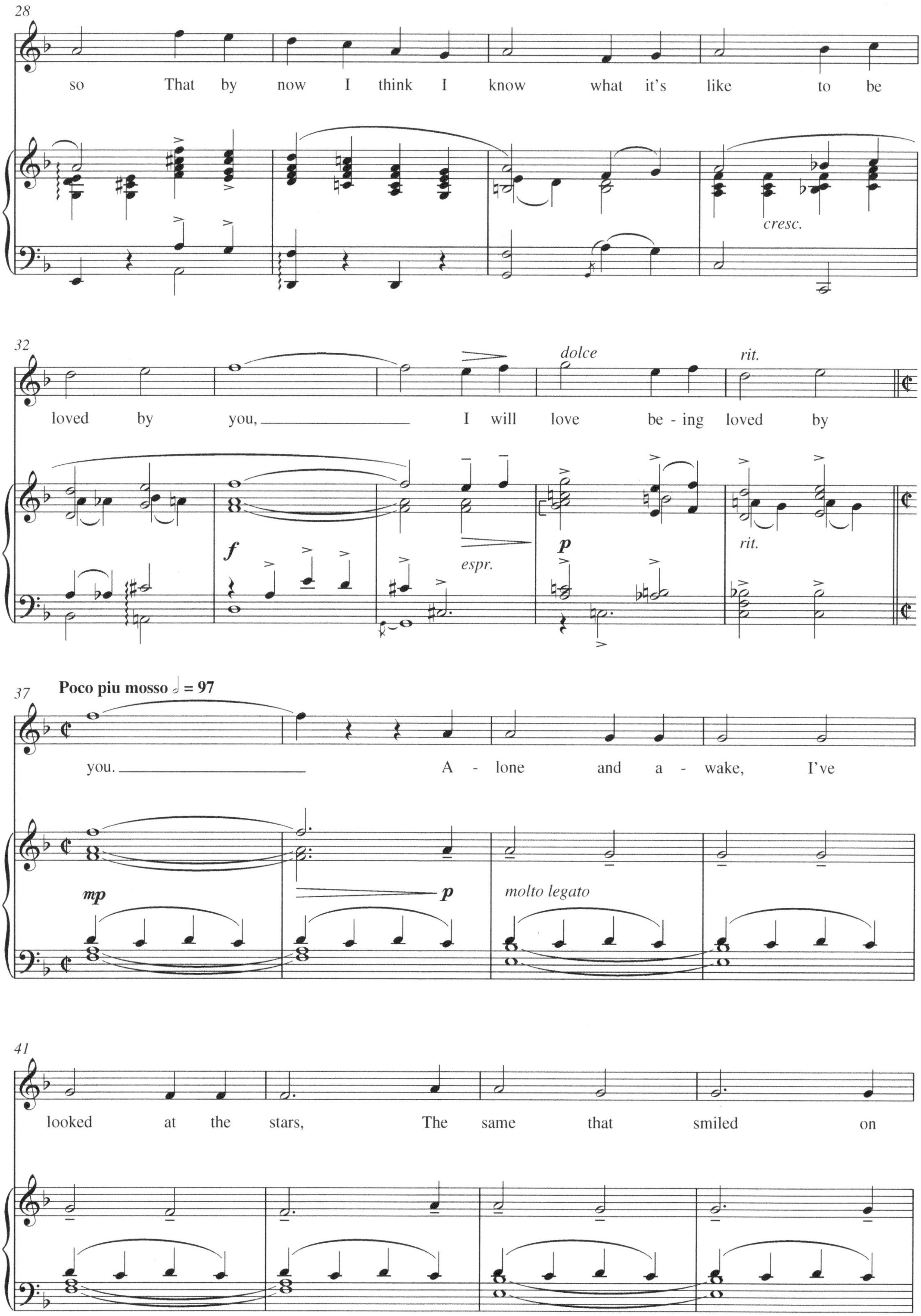
28
so That by now I think I know what it's like to be
cresc.
32
dolce
rit.
loved by you, I will love be - ing loved by
f
espr.
p
rit.
37
Poco piu mosso 𝅗𝅥 = 97
you. A - lone and a - wake, I've
mp
p
molto legato
41
looked at the stars, The same that smiled on

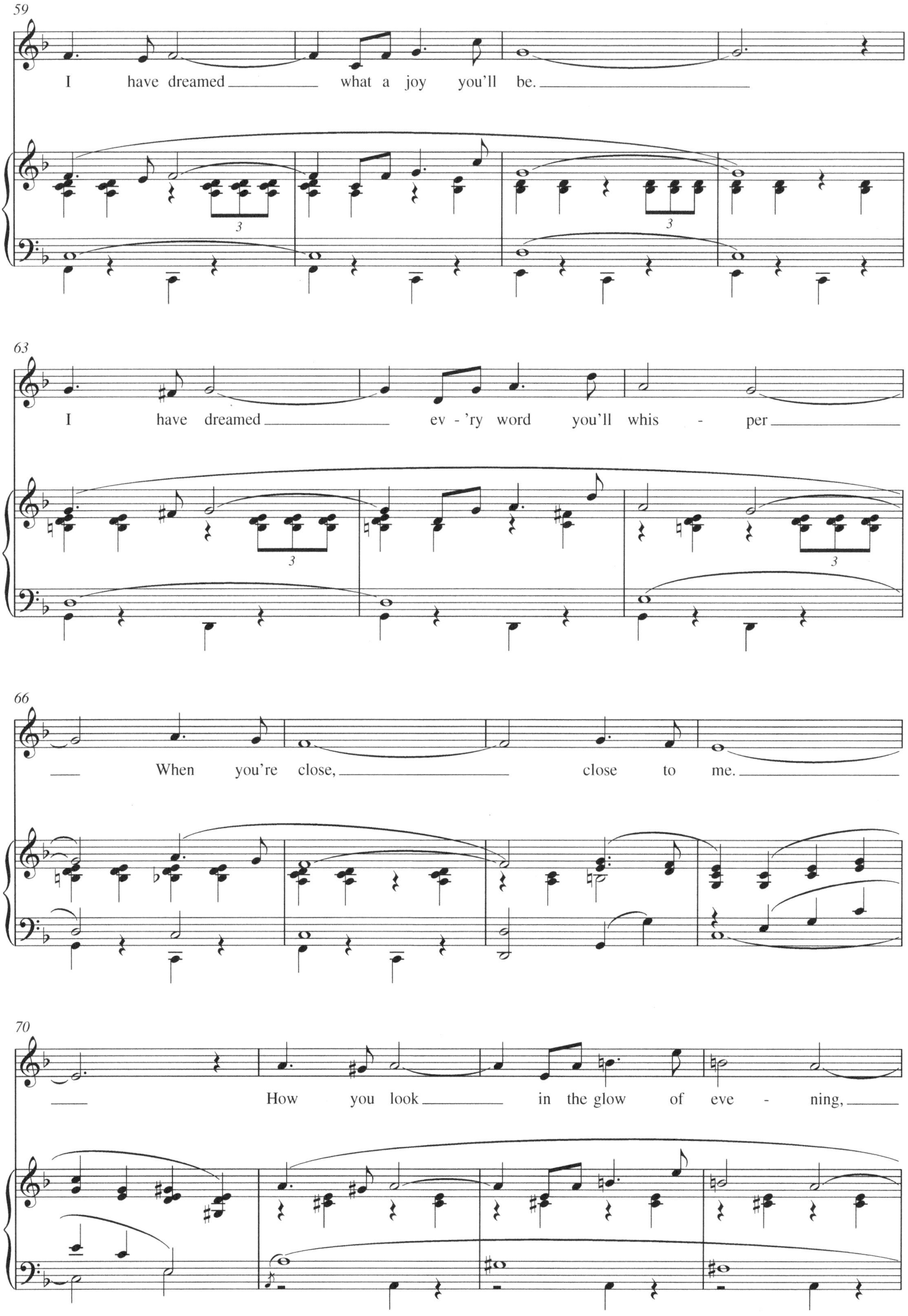
59
I have dreamed what a joy you'll be.
63
I have dreamed ev - 'ry word you'll whis - per
66
When you're close, close to me.
70
How you look in the glow of eve - ning,

# BAUBLES, BANGLES AND BEADS
## from *Kismet*

Words and Music by
Robert Wright and George Forrest
(Music Based on Themes of A. Borodin)

*Marsinah is joined by the chorus in the show, adapted here as a solo.*

Copyright © 1953 Frank Music Corp.
Copyright Renewed and Assigned to Scheffel Music Corp., New York, NY
All Rights Controlled by Scheffel Music Corp.
All Rights Reserved   Used by Permission

# AND THIS IS MY BELOVED
from *Kismet*

Words and Music by
Robert Wright and George Forrest
(Music Based on themes of A. Borodin)

Copyright © 1953 Frank Music Corp.
Copyright Renewed and Assigned to Scheffel Music Corp., New York, NY
All Rights Controlled by Scheffel Music Corp.
All Rights Reserved   Used by Permission

# CHILDREN WILL LISTEN
from *Into the Woods*

Words and Music by
Stephen Sondheim

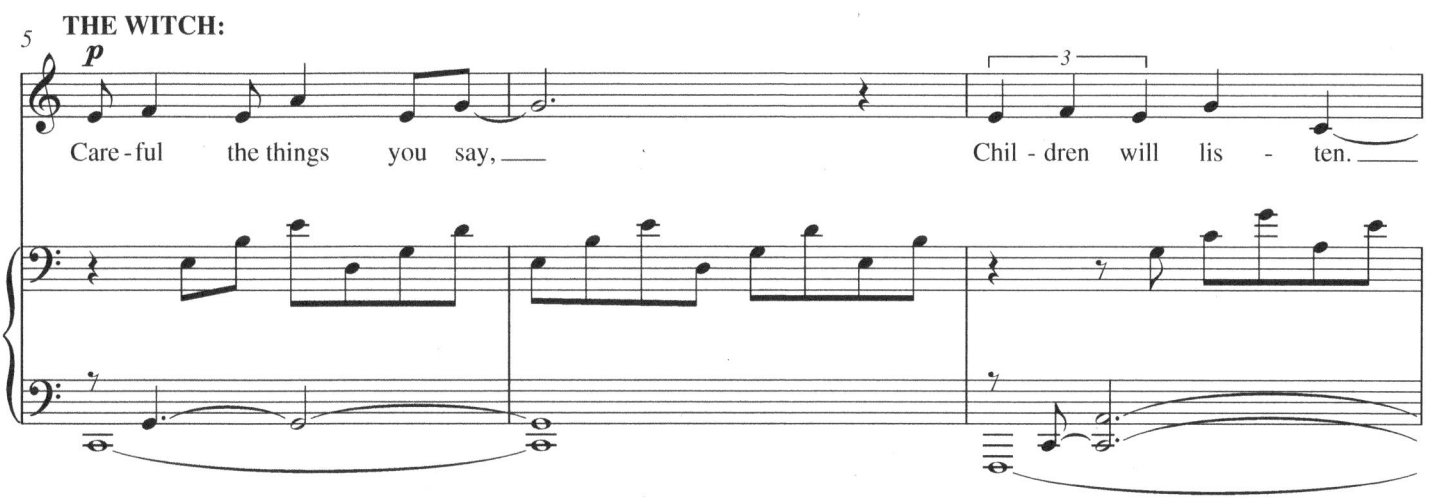

*This song is an ensemble number in the show, adapted as a solo for this edition.*

© 1988 RILTING MUSIC, INC.
All Rights Administered by WB MUSIC CORP.
All Rights Reserved Used By Permission

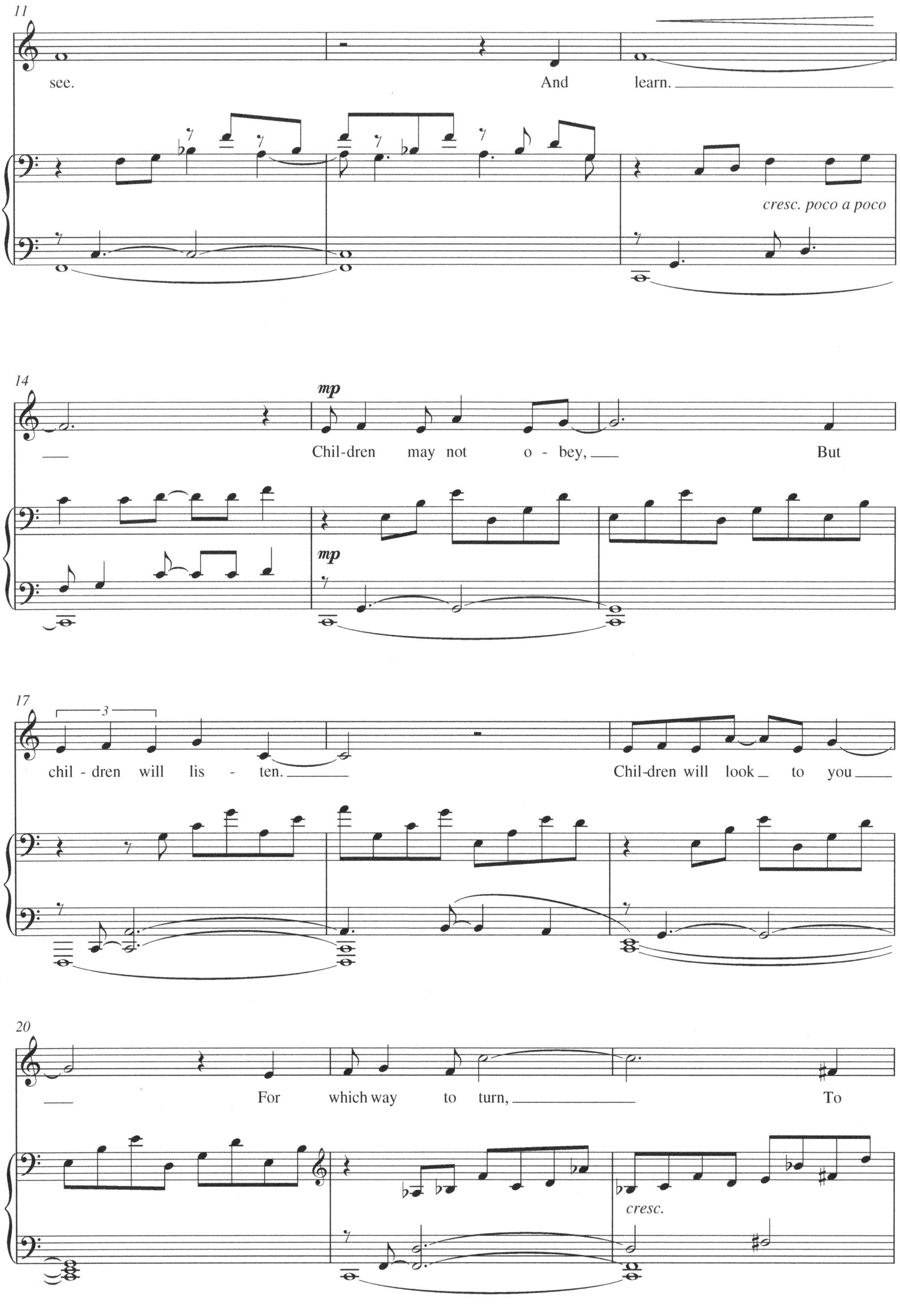
11
see.
And learn.
cresc. poco a poco
14
mp
Chil-dren may not o - bey,
But
mp
17
3
chil - dren will lis - ten.
Chil-dren will look to you
20
For which way to turn,
To
cresc.

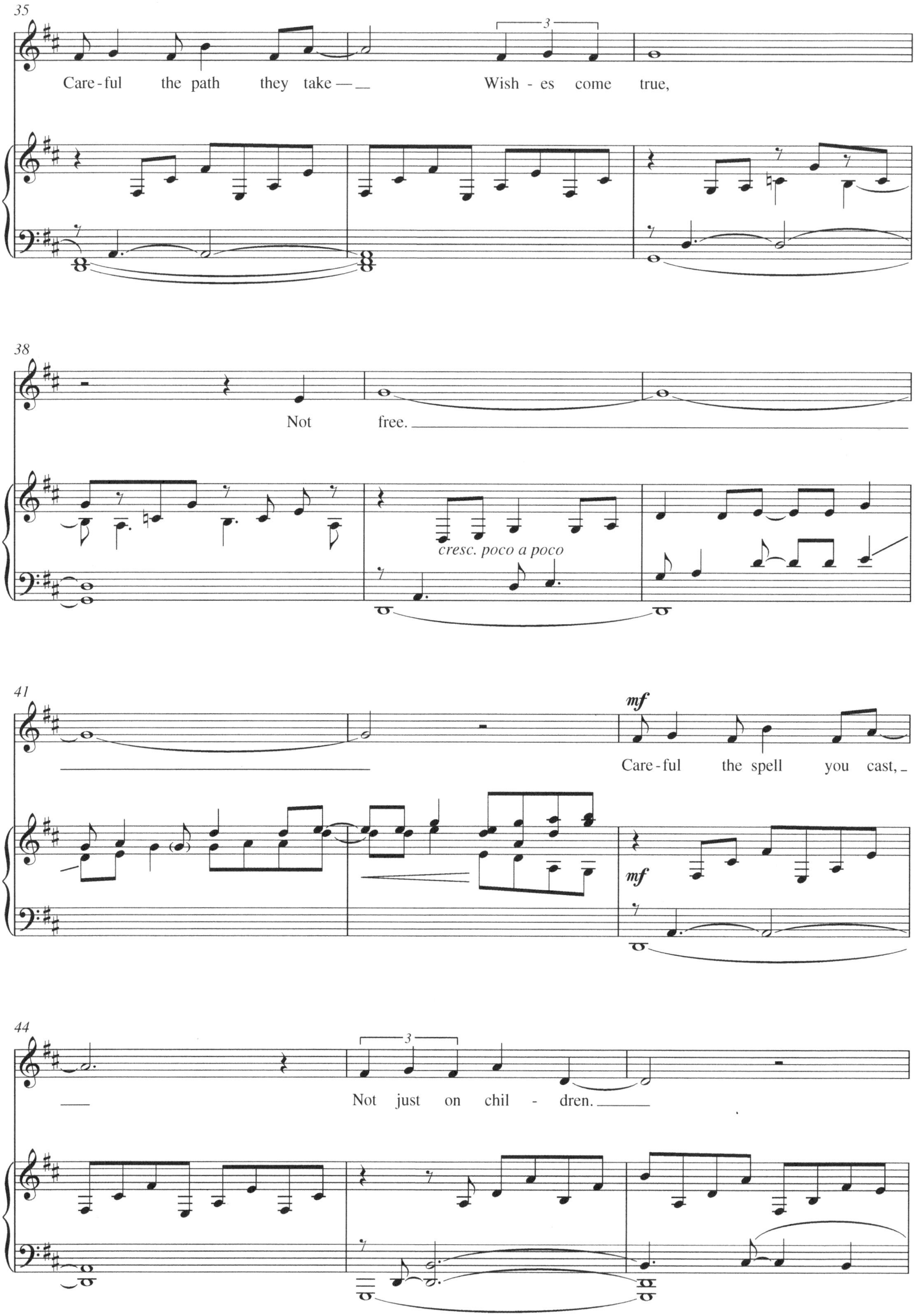
35
Care - ful the path they take — Wish - es come true,
38
Not free.
cresc. poco a poco
41
mf
Care - ful the spell you cast, Not just on chil - dren.
mf
44

# SO IN LOVE
from *Kiss Me, Kate*

Words and Music by
Cole Porter

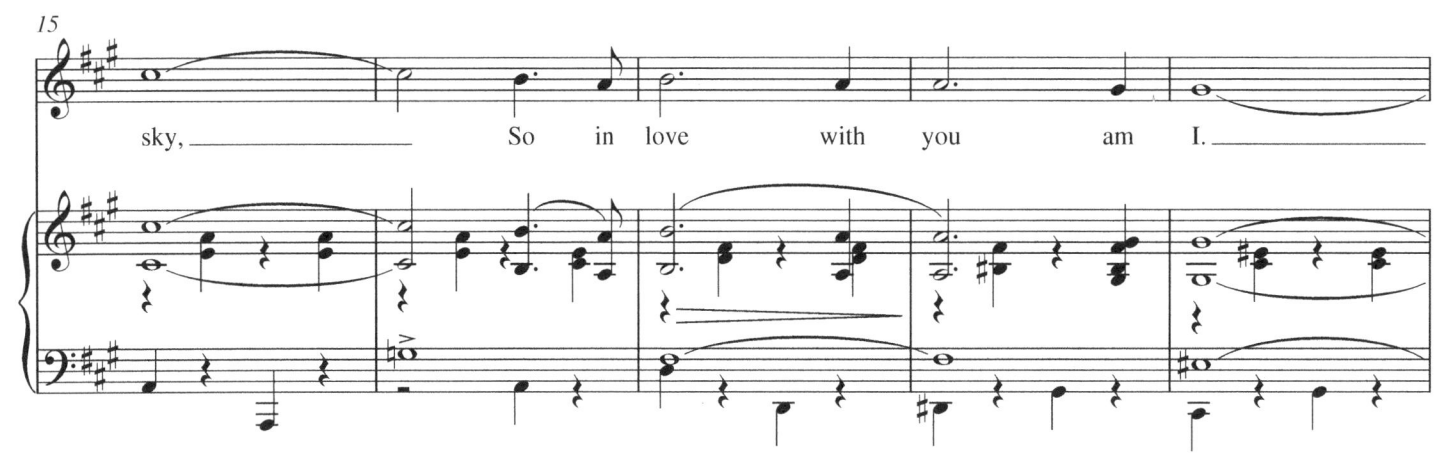

Copyright © 1948 by Cole Porter
Copyright Renewed, Assigned to John F. Wharton, Trustee of the Cole Porter Musical and Literary Property Trusts
Chappell & Co. owner of publication and allied rights throughout the world
International Copyright Secured   All Rights Reserved

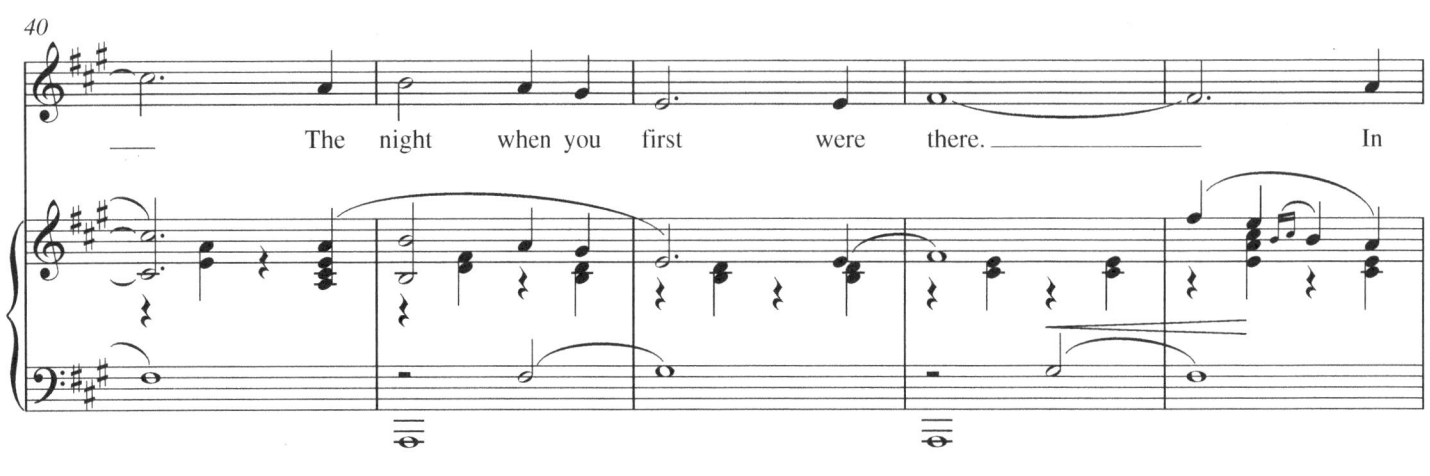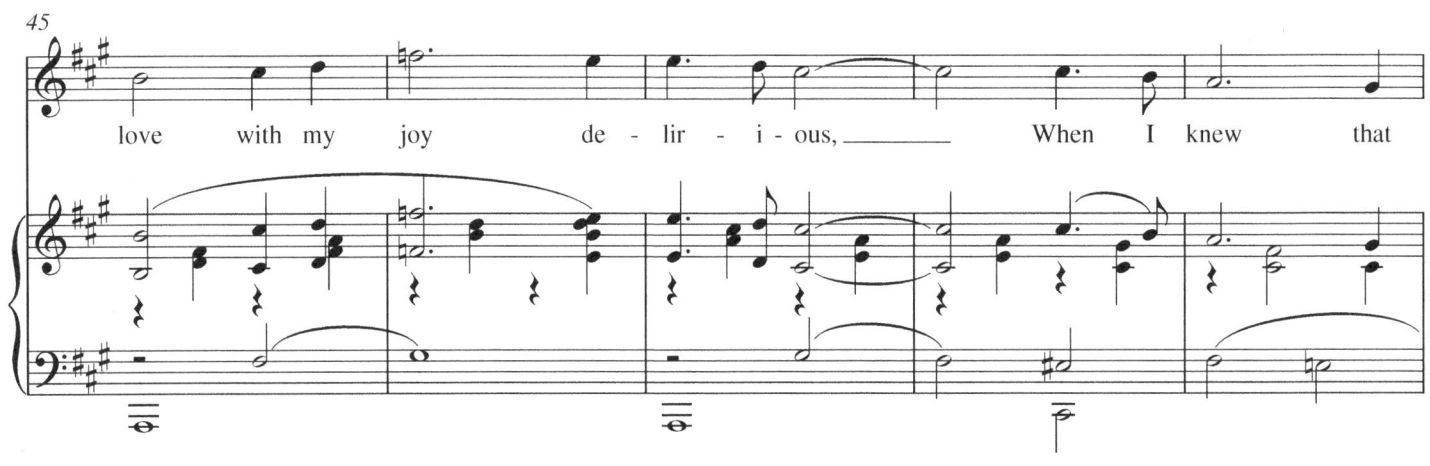

# MY SHIP
## from the Musical Production *Lady in the Dark*

Words by Ira Gershwin
Music by Kurt Weill

# THE BEAUTY IS
from *The Light in the Piazza*

Words and Music by
Adam Guettel

These are ver-y pop-u-lar in It-a-ly!

Copyright © 2005 MATTHEW MUSIC
Publishing and Allied Rights Administered by WILLIAMSON MUSIC throughout the world
International Copyright Secured   All Rights Reserved

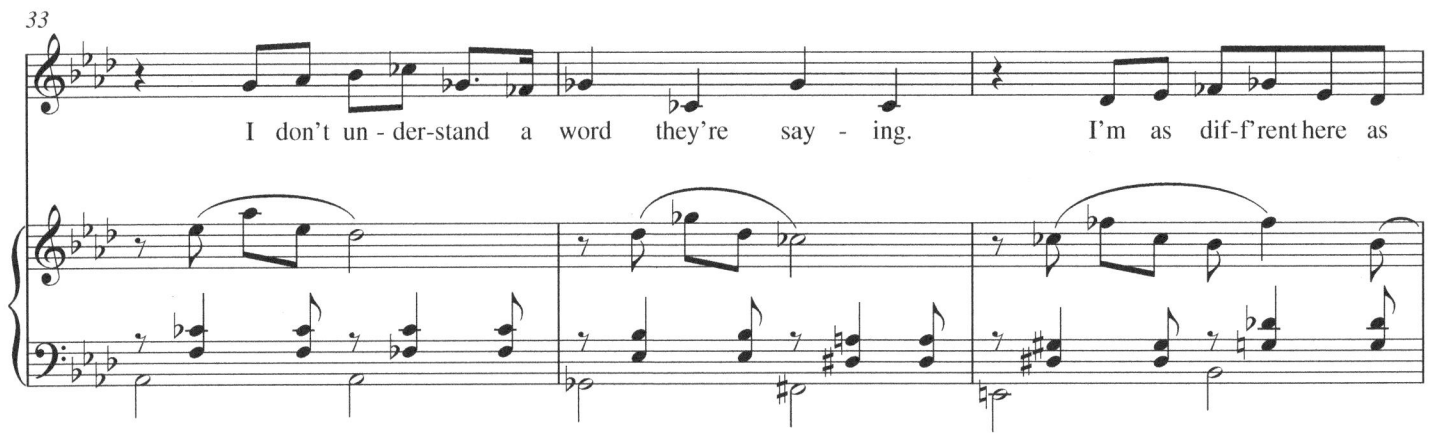

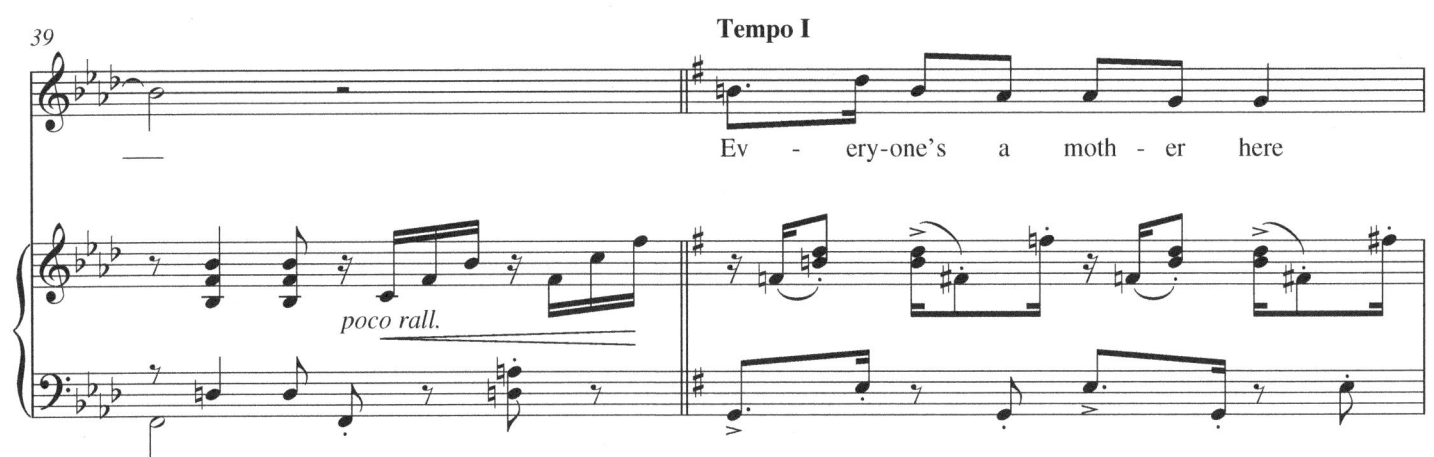

# NO OTHER LOVE
## from *Me and Juliet*

Lyrics by Oscar Hammerstein II
Music by Richard Rodgers

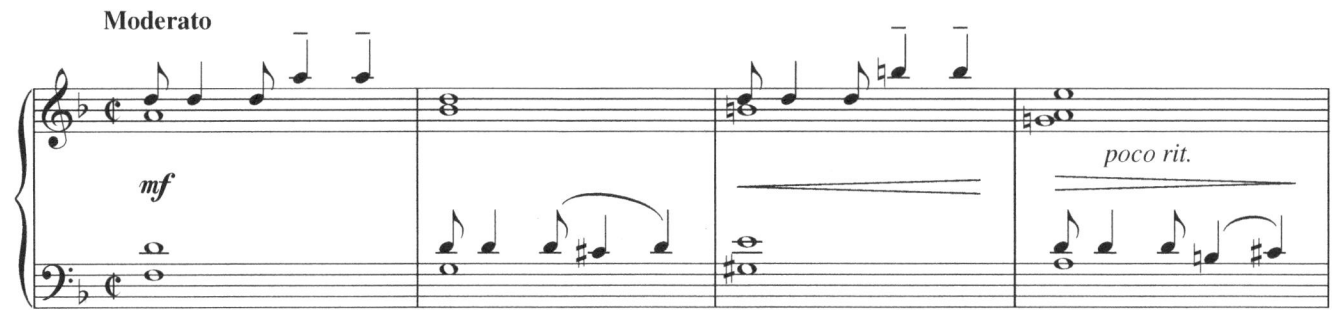

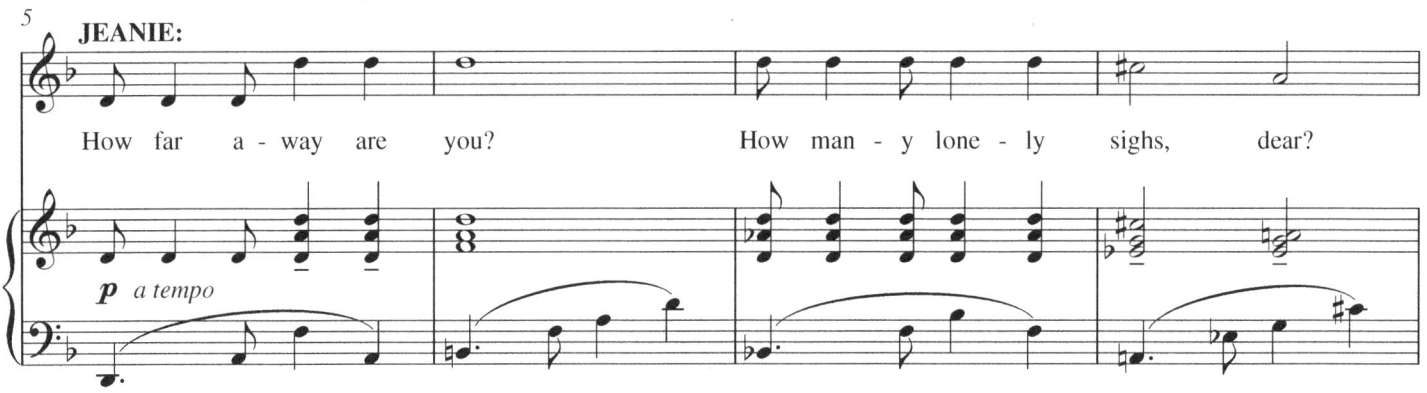

Copyright © 1953 by Richard Rodgers and Oscar Hammerstein II
Copyright Renewed
WILLIAMSON MUSIC owner of publication and allied rights throughout the world
International Copyright Secured   All Rights Reserved

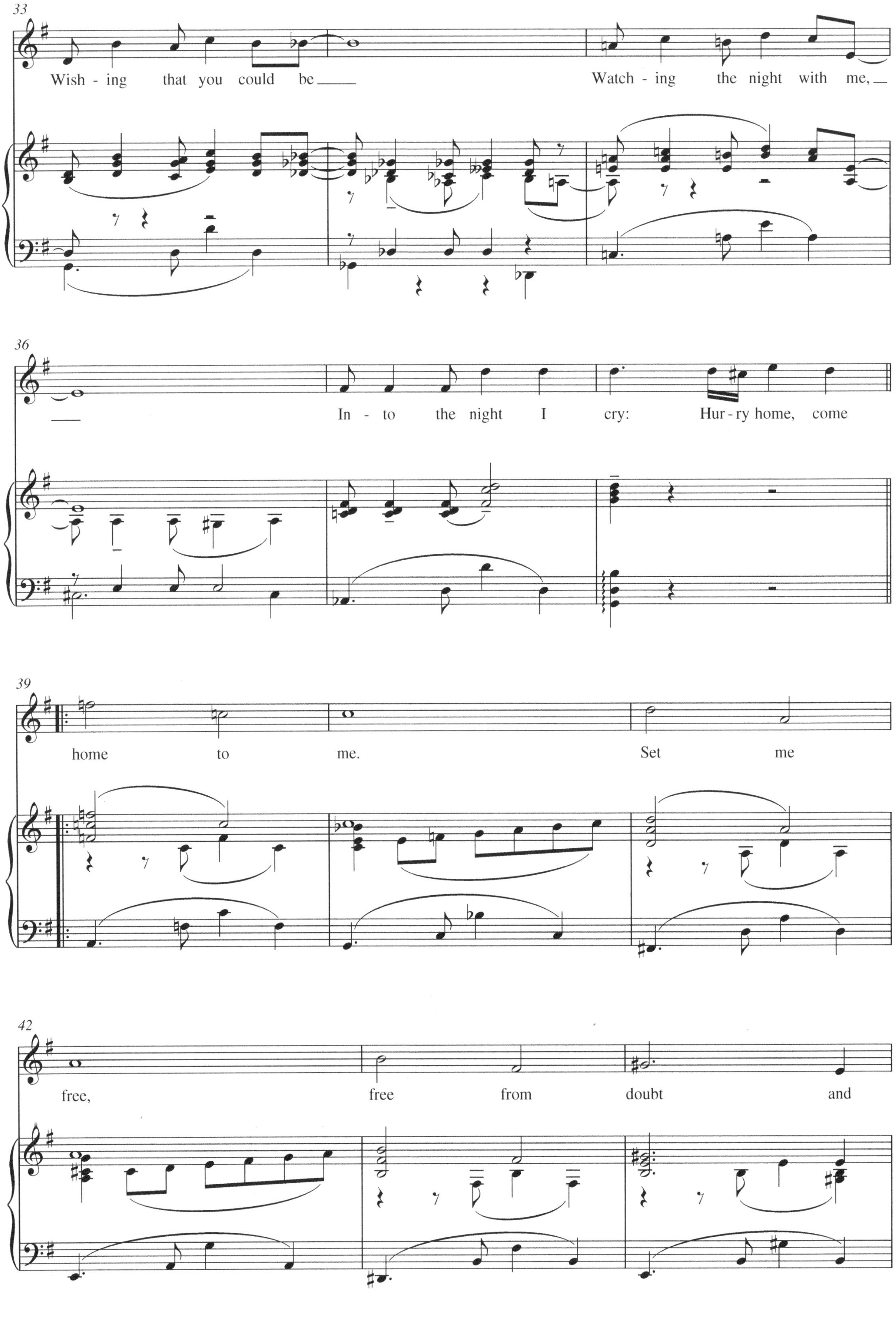
33
Wish - ing that you could be
Watch - ing the night with me,
36
In - to the night I cry: Hur - ry home, come
39
home to me.
Set me
42
free,
free from doubt and

# SOMEBODY, SOMEWHERE
from *The Most Happy Fella*

By Frank Loesser

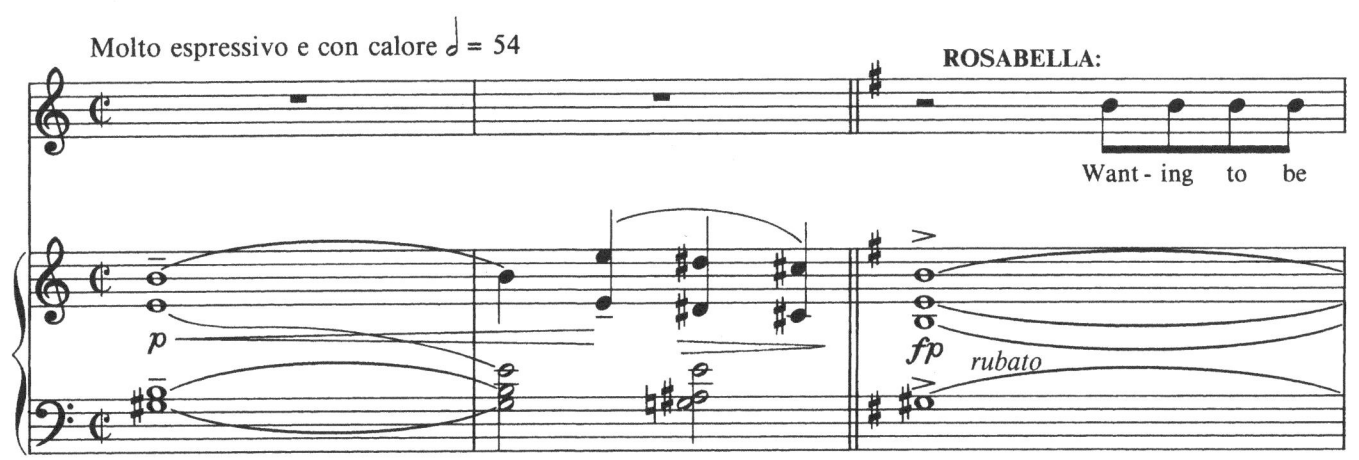

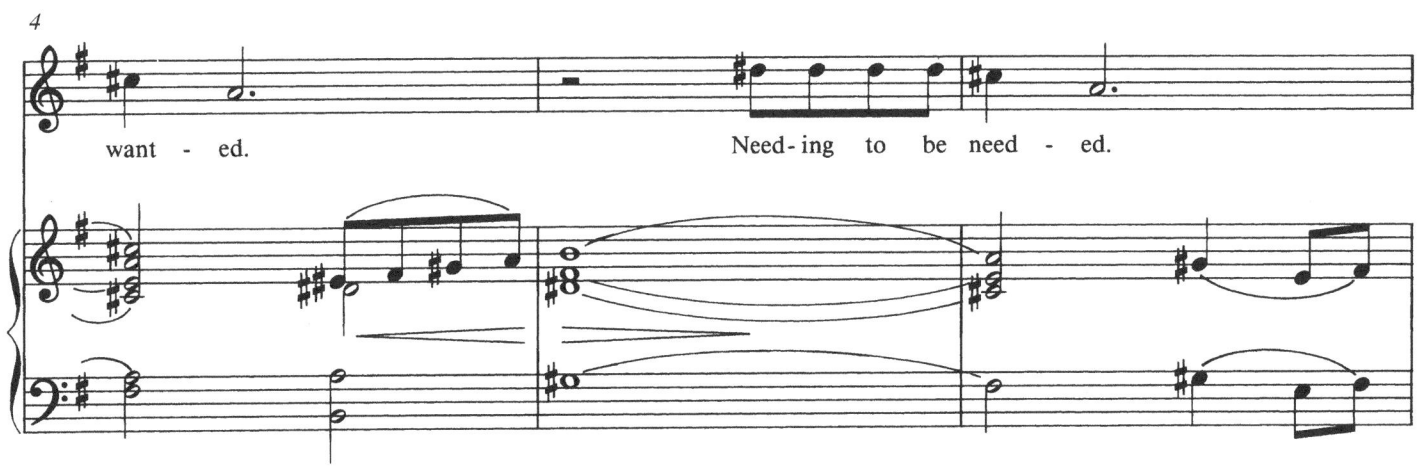

© 1956 (Renewed) FRANK MUSIC CORP.
All Rights Reserved

# NOT A DAY GOES BY
from *Merrily We Roll Along*

Words and Music by
Stephen Sondheim

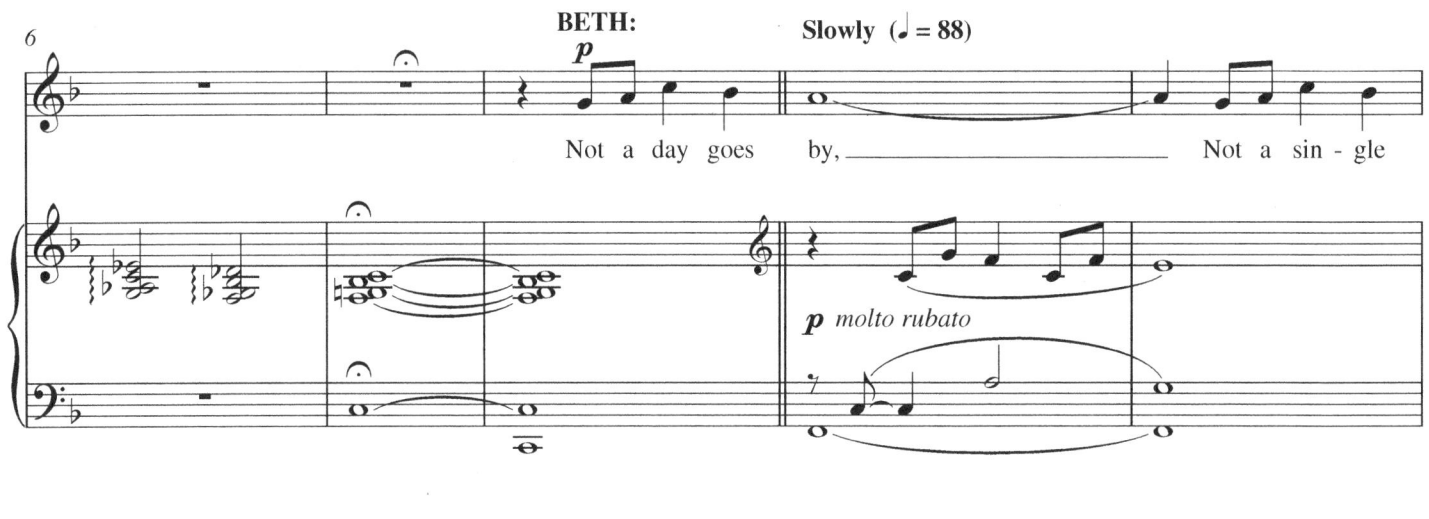
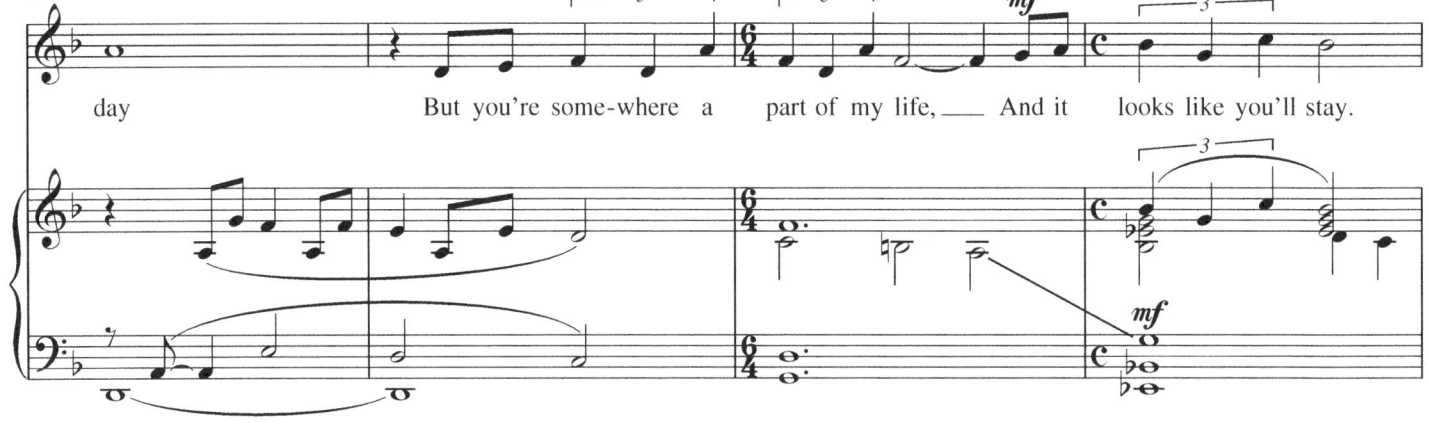

© 1981 RILTING MUSIC, INC.
All Rights Administered by WB MUSIC CORP.
All Rights Reserved    Used by Permission

# THE SONG IS YOU
from *Music in the Air*

Lyrics by Oscar Hammerstein II
Music by Jerome Kern

Transposed up for this edition. Original key: C Major.

Copyright © 1932 UNIVERSAL - POLYGRAM INTERNATIONAL PUBLISHING, INC.
Copyright Renewed
All Rights Reserved  Used by Permission

# GOODNIGHT, MY SOMEONE
from Meredith Willson's *The Music Man*

By Meredith Willson

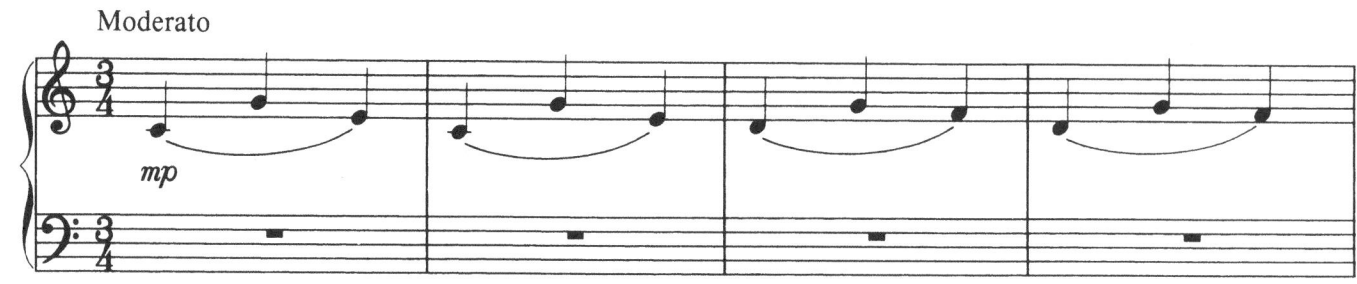
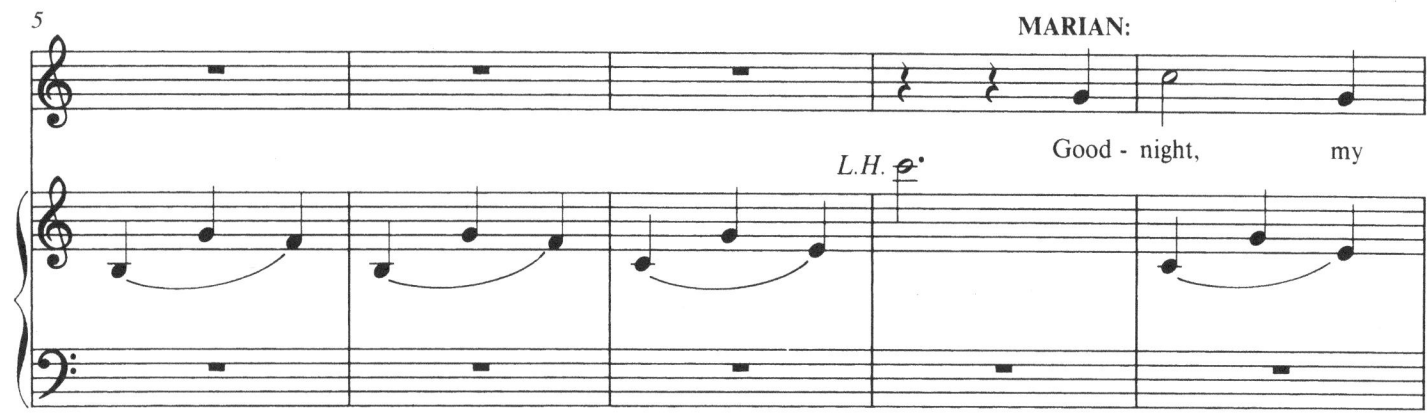

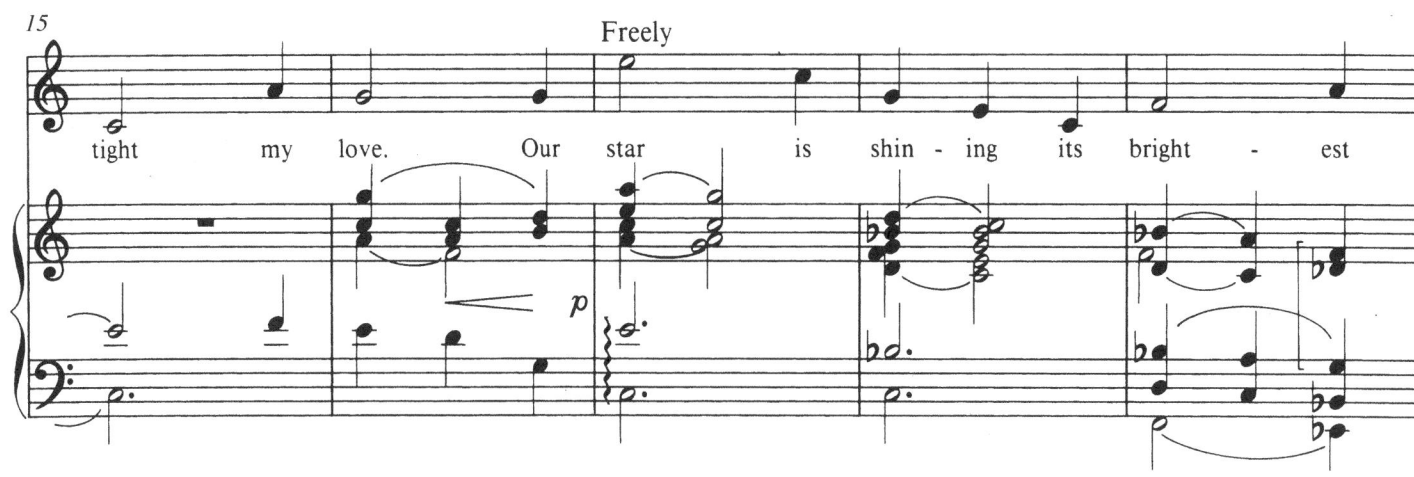

© 1957 (Renewed) FRANK MUSIC CORP. and MEREDITH WILLSON MUSIC
All Rights Reserved

# TILL THERE WAS YOU
## from Meredith Willson's *The Music Man*

By Meredith Willson

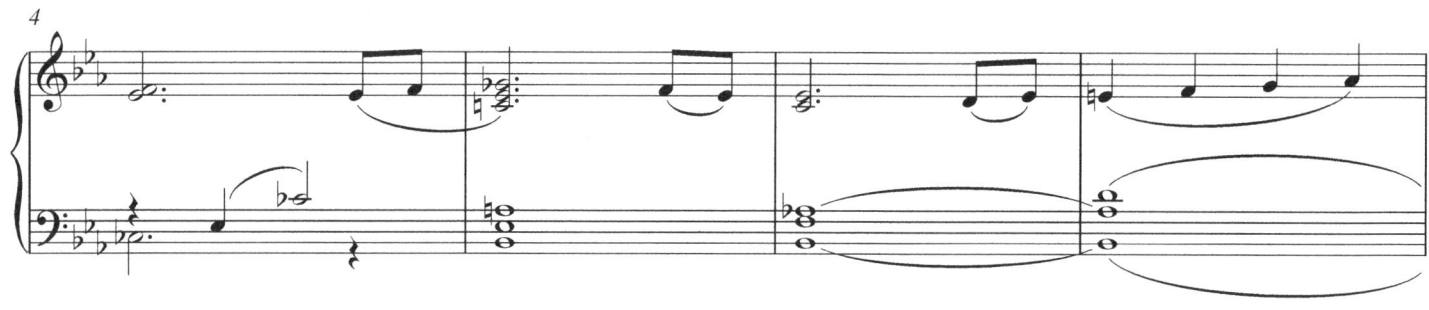
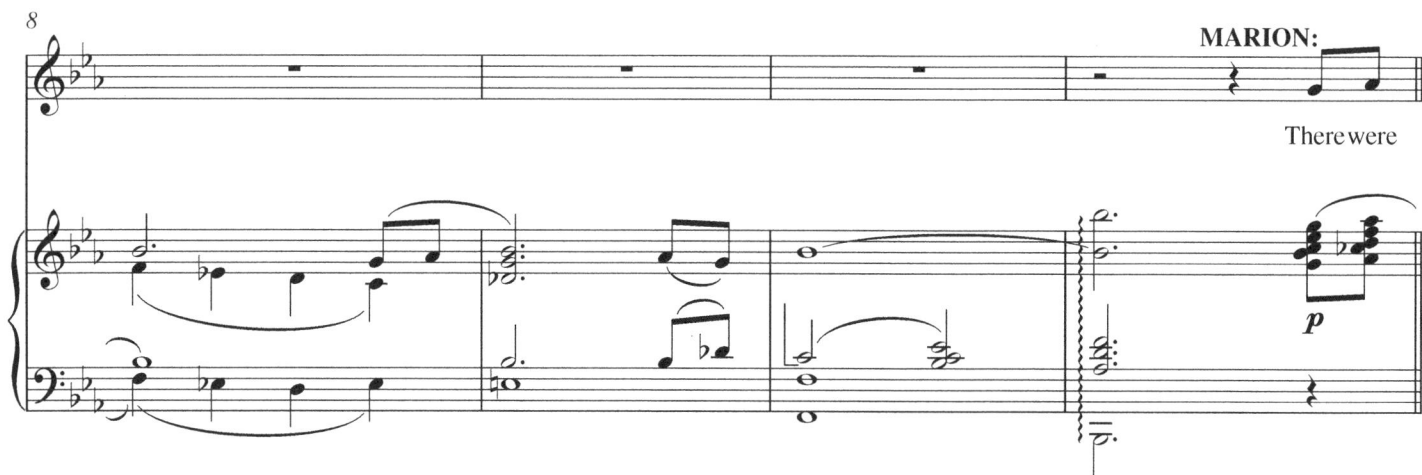

© 1950, 1957 (Renewed) FRANK MUSIC CORP. and MEREDITH WILLSON MUSIC
All Rights Reserved

126

# I COULD HAVE DANCED ALL NIGHT
from *My Fair Lady*

Words by Alan Jay Lerner
Music by Frederick Loewe

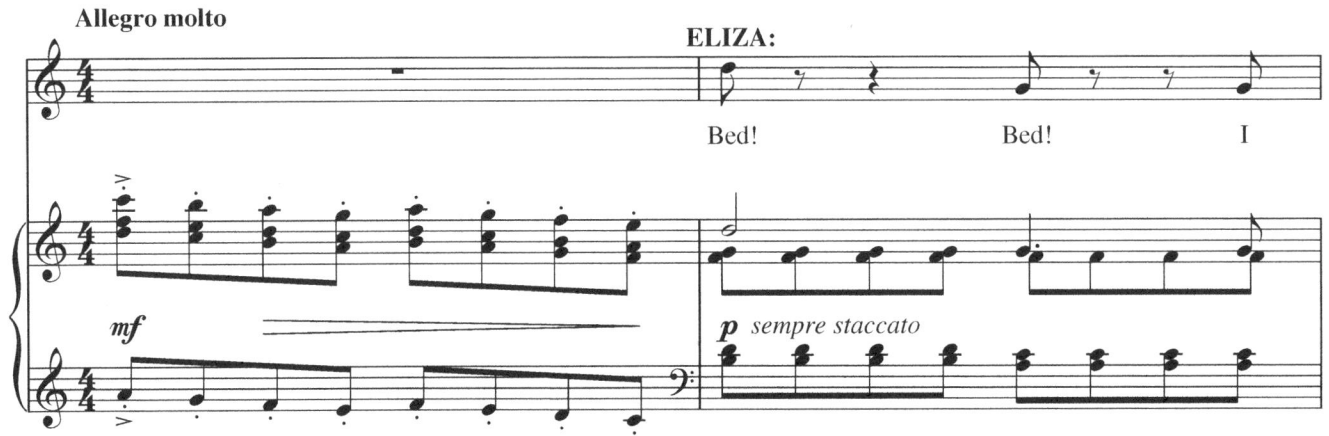

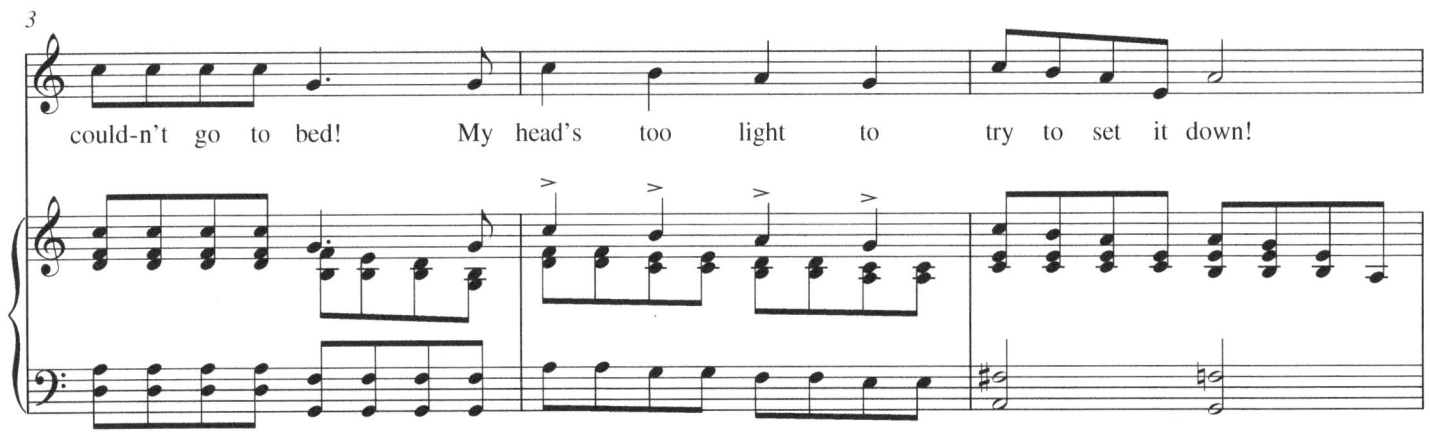

Copyright © 1956 by Alan Jay Lerner and Frederick Loewe
Copyright Renewed
Chappell & Co., owner of publication and allied rights throughout the world
International Copyright Secured  All Rights Reserved

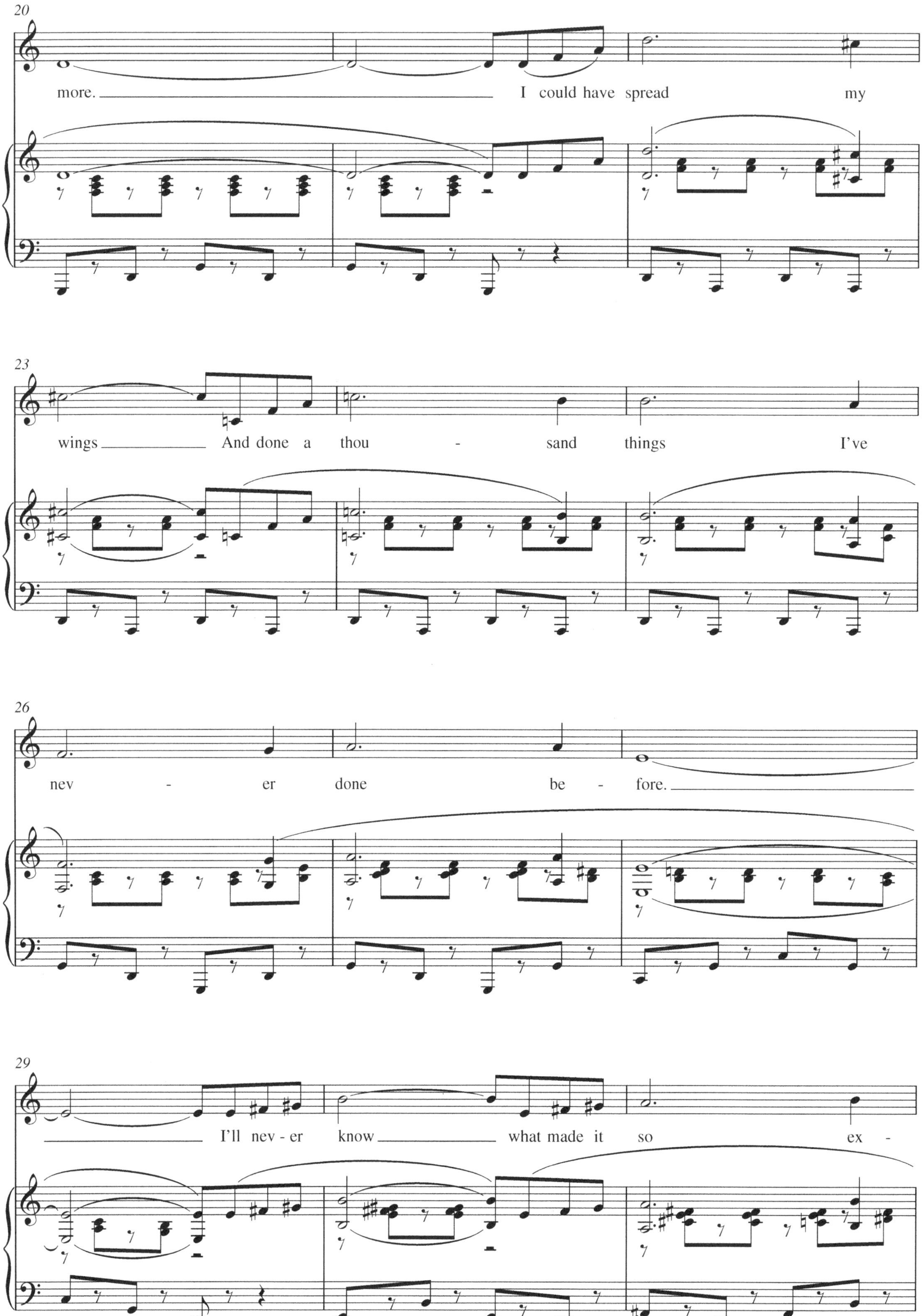
20
more.
I could have spread my
23
wings
And done a thou - sand things I've
26
nev - er done be - fore.
29
I'll nev - er know what made it so ex -

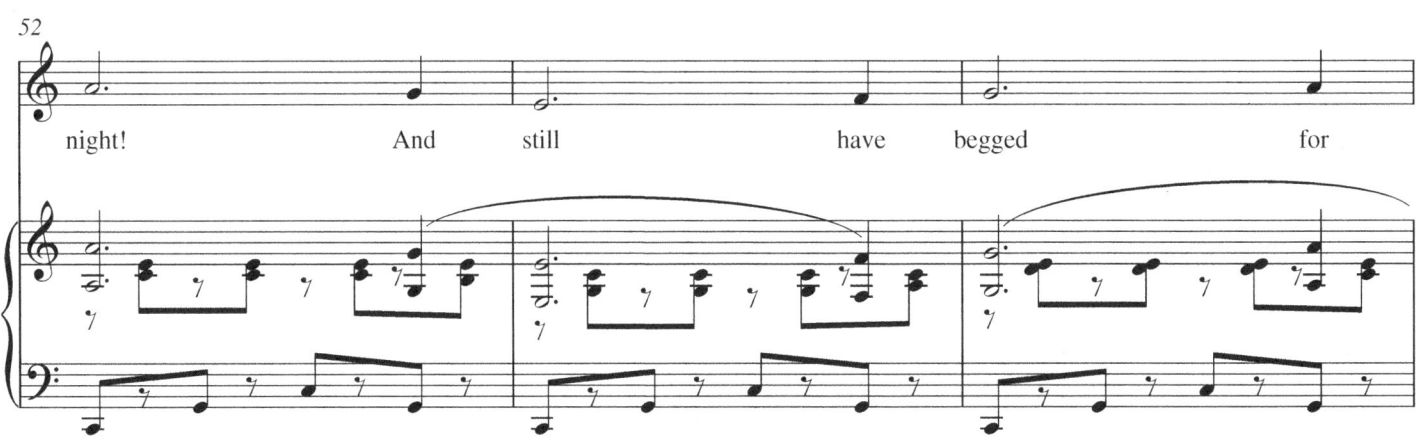
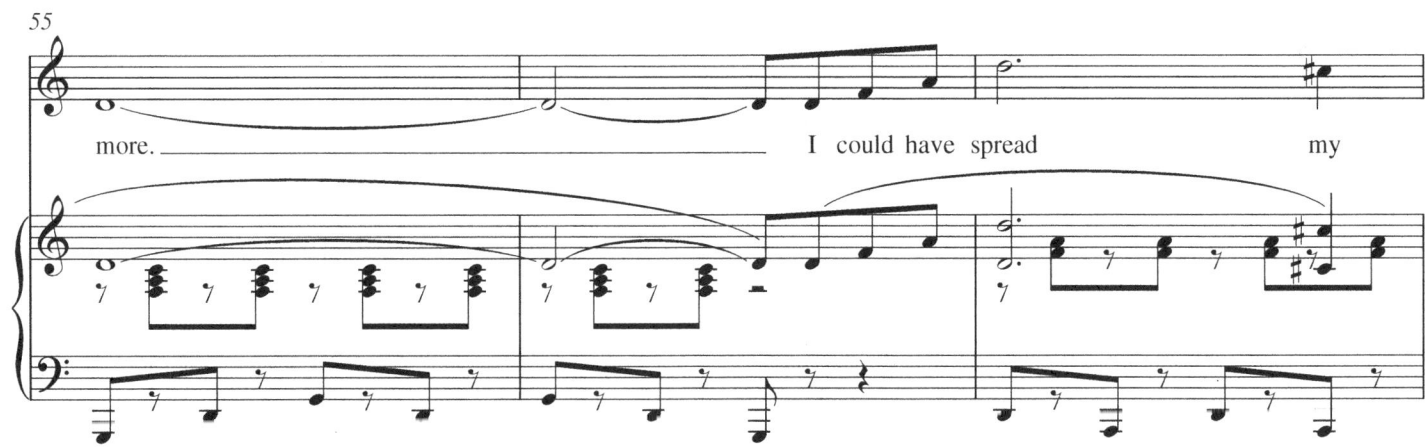

# SHOW ME
## from *My Fair Lady*

Words by Alan Jay Lerner
Music by Frederick Loewe

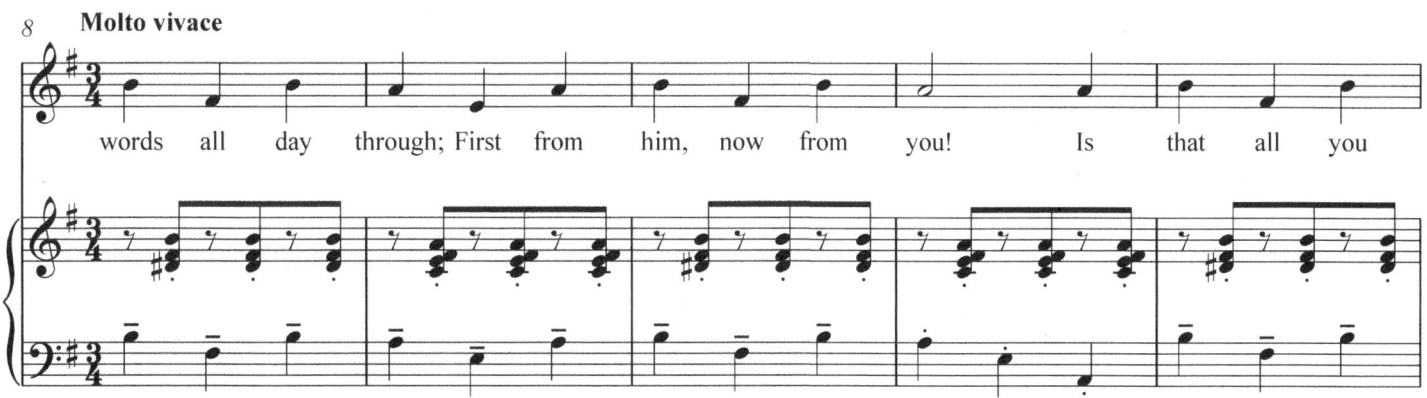

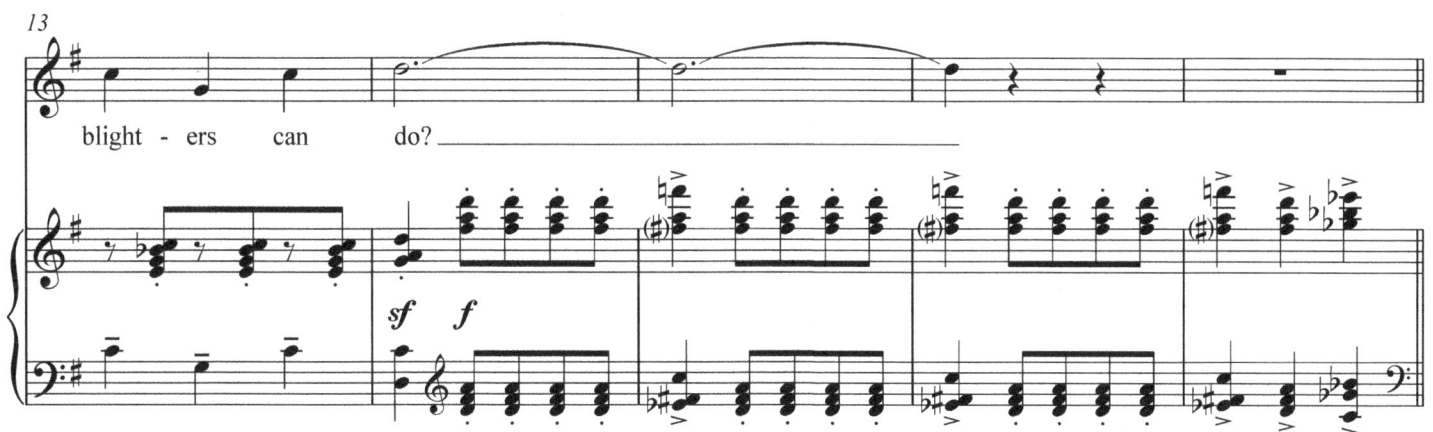

Copyright © 1956 by Alan Jay Lerner and Frederick Loewe
Copyright Renewed
Chappell & Co. owner of publication and allied rights throughout the world
International Copyright Secured   All Rights Reserved

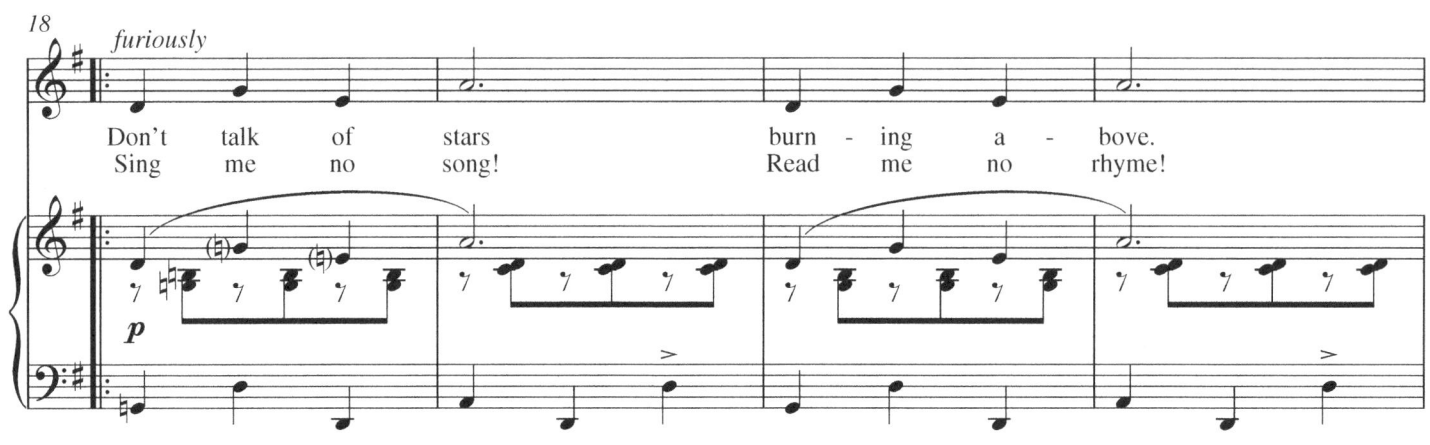
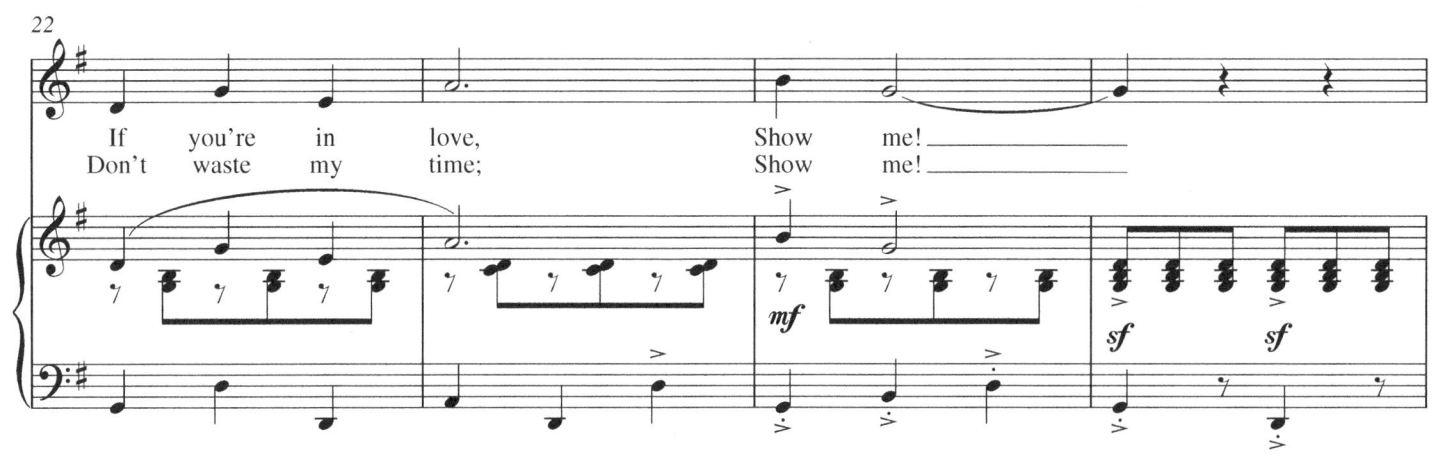

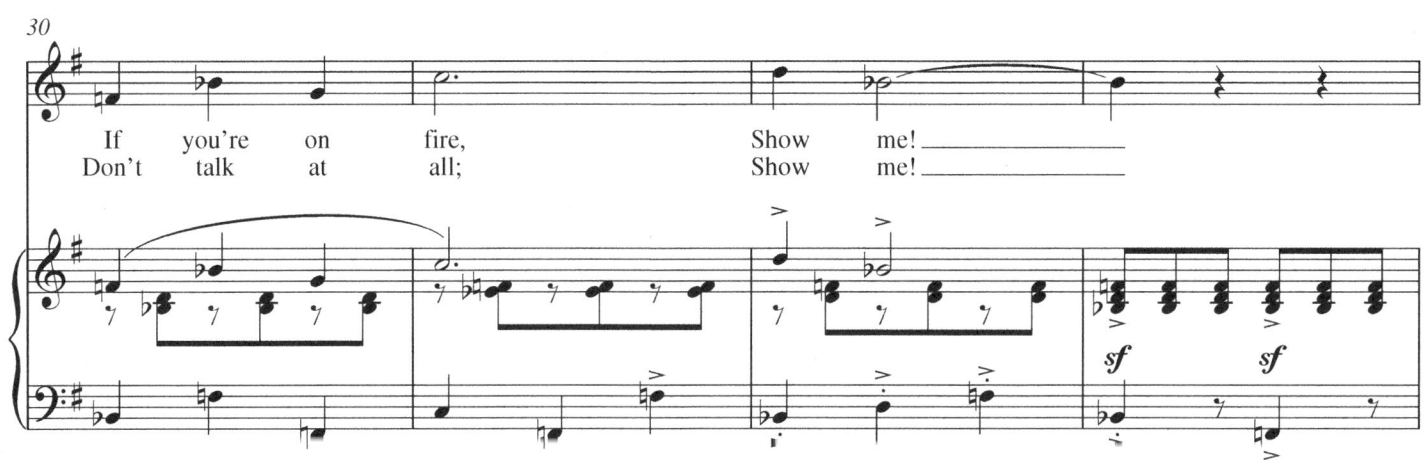

49
Have - n't your lips longed for my
Have - n't your arms hun - gered for
p subito
53
touch? Don't say how much; Show me!
mine? Please don't ex - pl'in; Show me!
mf
57
Show me! Don't talk of
Show me! Don't wait un -
sf
sf
sf
sf
61
love last - ing through time. Make me no
til wrin - kles and lines pop out all

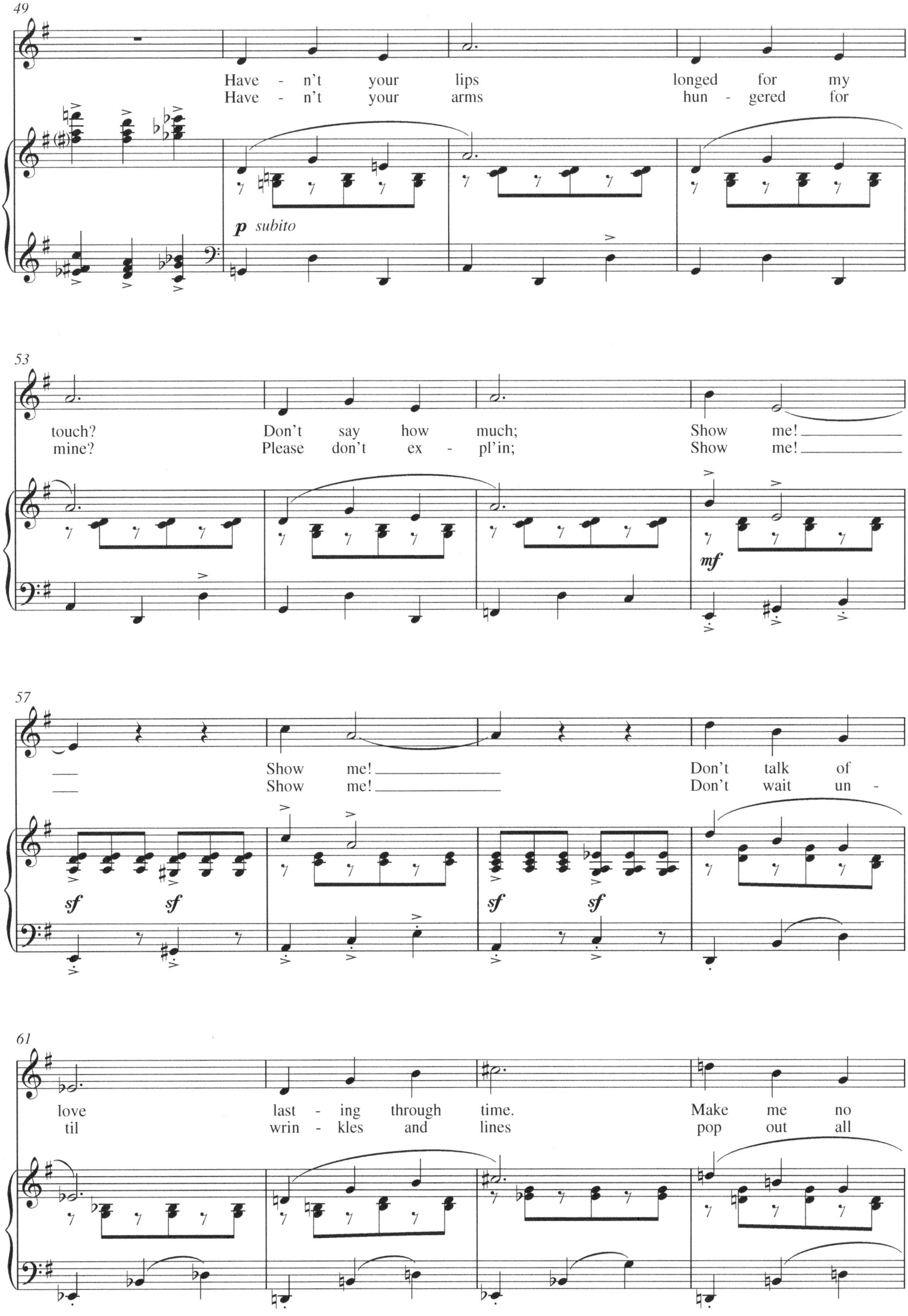

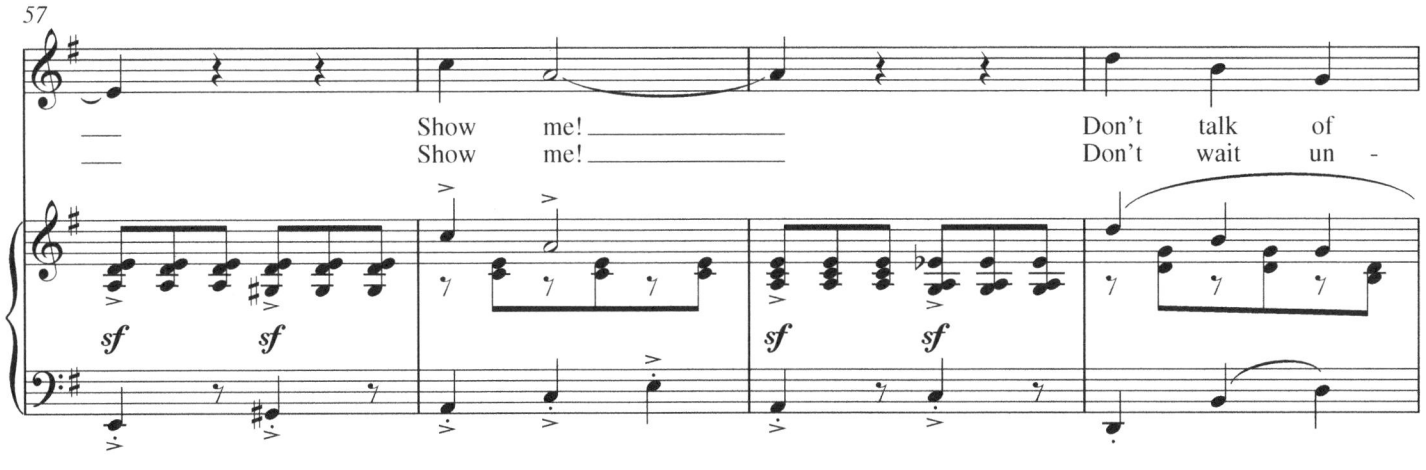

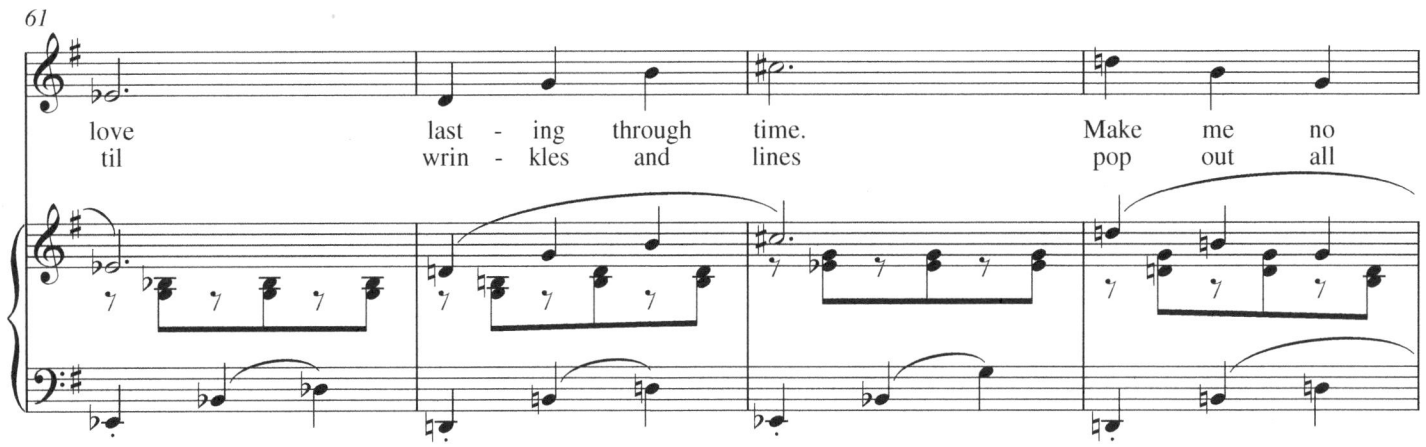

# MOONFALL
## from *The Mystery of Edwin Drood*

Words and Music by
Rupert Holmes

© 1986 THE HOLMES LINE OF RECORDS, INC.
All Rights Reserved

# OLD MAID
from *110 in the Shade*

Words by Tom Jones
Music by Harvey Schmidt

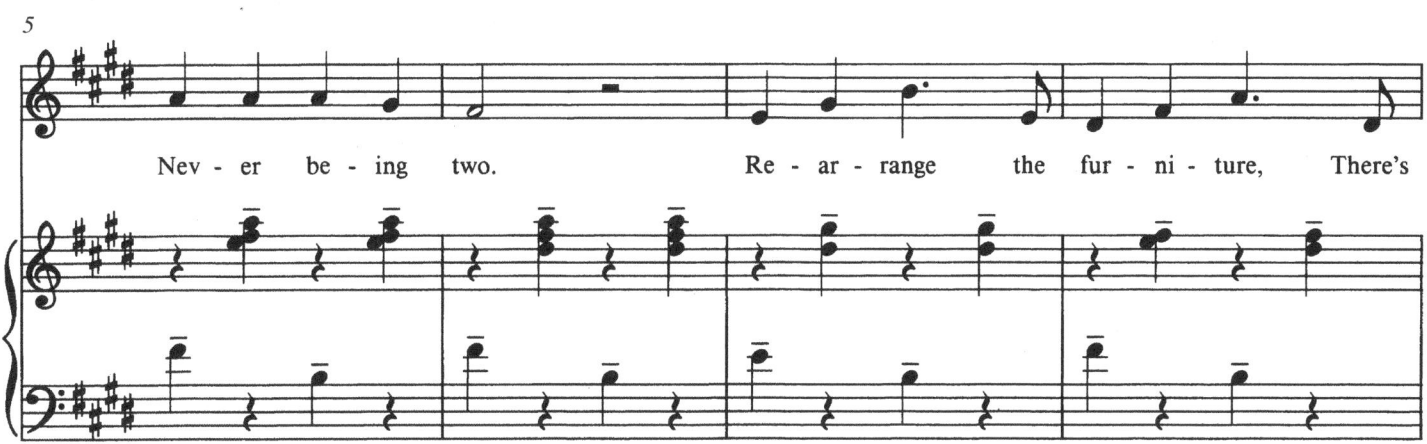

Copyright © 1963 by Tom Jones and Harvey Schmidt
Copyright Renewed
Portfolio Music, Inc., owner, and Chappell & Co., administrator of publication and allied rights throughout the world
International Copyright Secured   All Rights Reserved

# OUT OF MY DREAMS
## from *Oklahoma!*

Lyrics by Oscar Hammerstein II
Music by Richard Rodgers

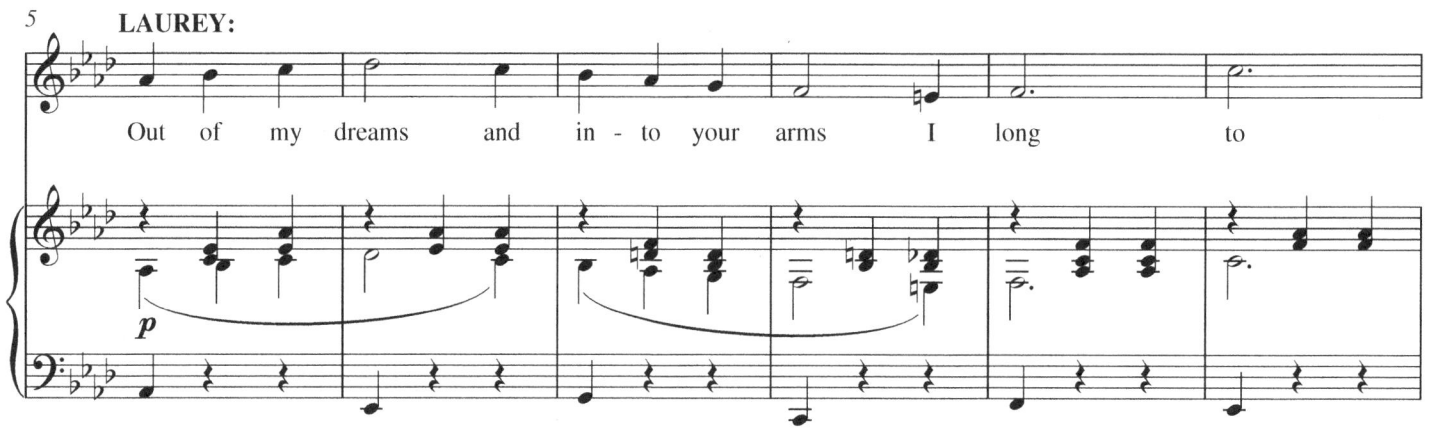

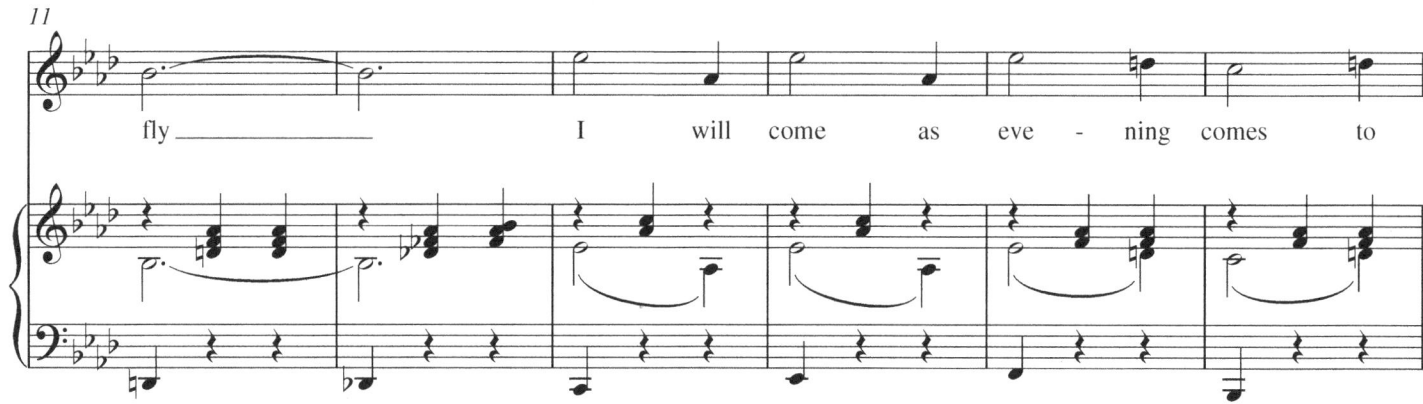

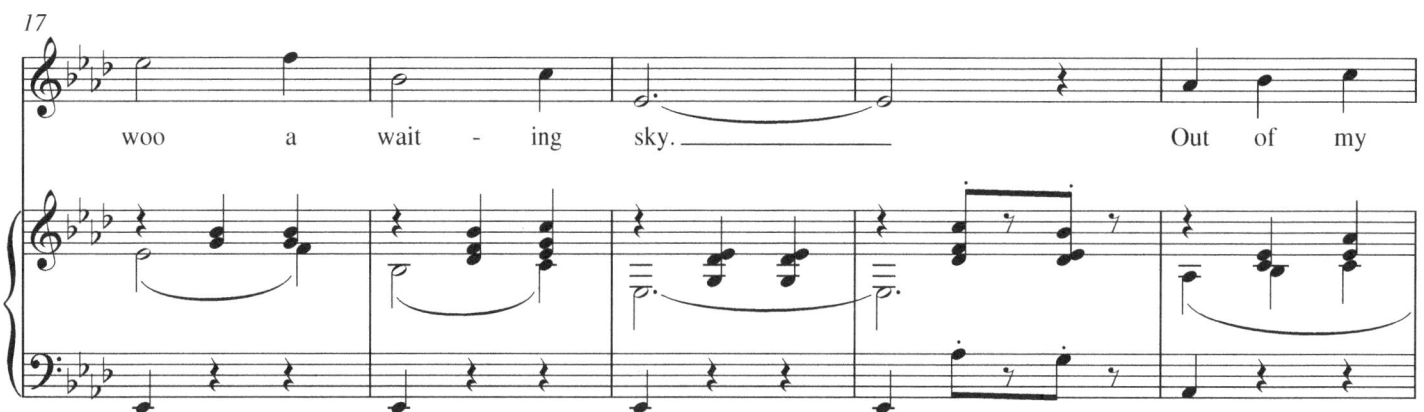

*This song appears in a somewhat different form here than in the context of the show.*
*Mr. Hammerstein revised the lyrics so that the song could stand alone; it is this revision that is used here.*

Copyright © 1943 by WILLIAMSON MUSIC
Copyright Renewed
International Copyright Secured   All Rights Reserved

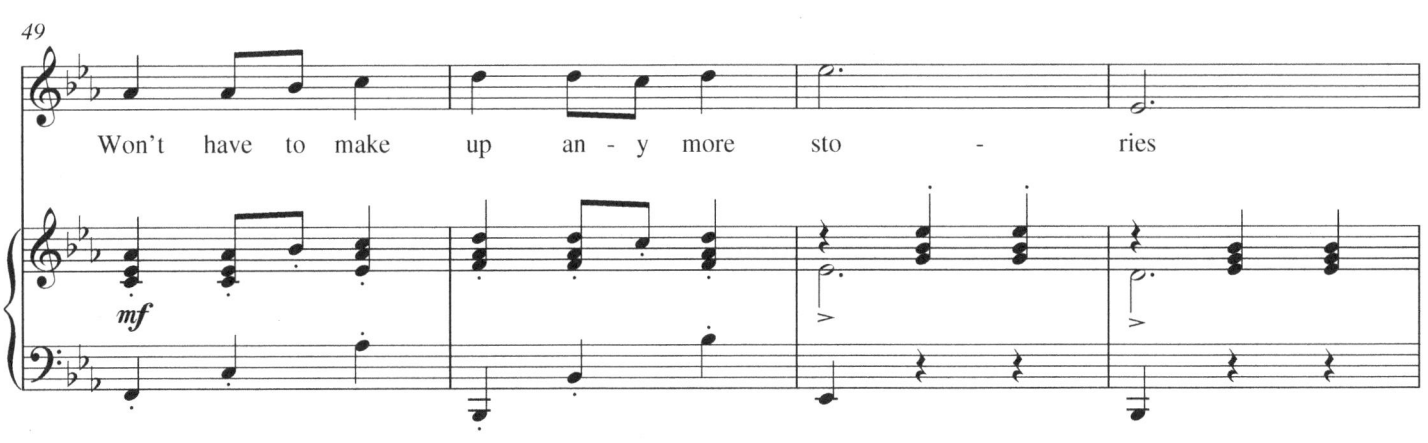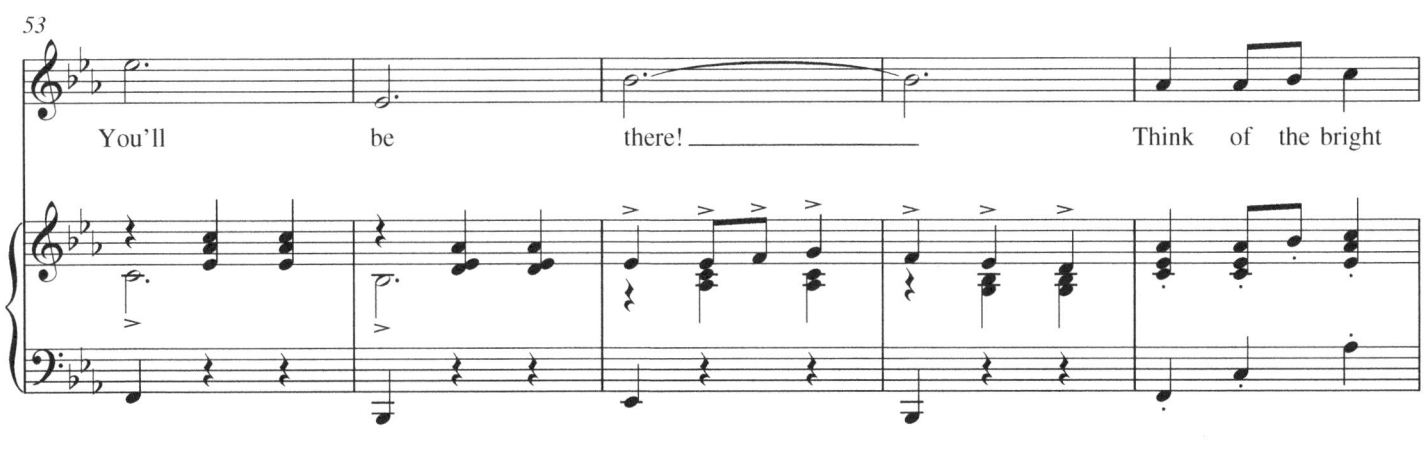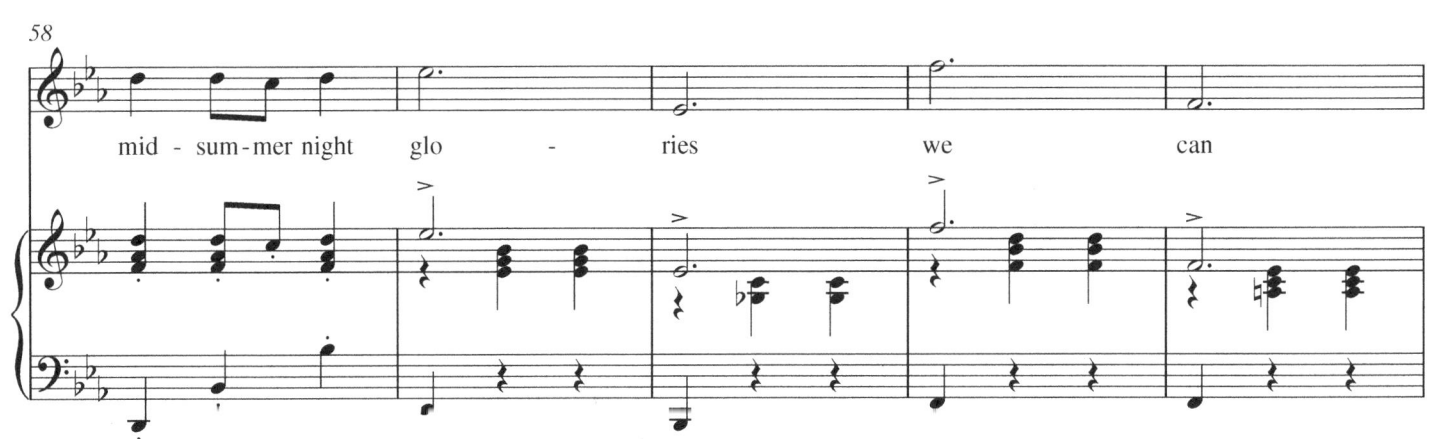

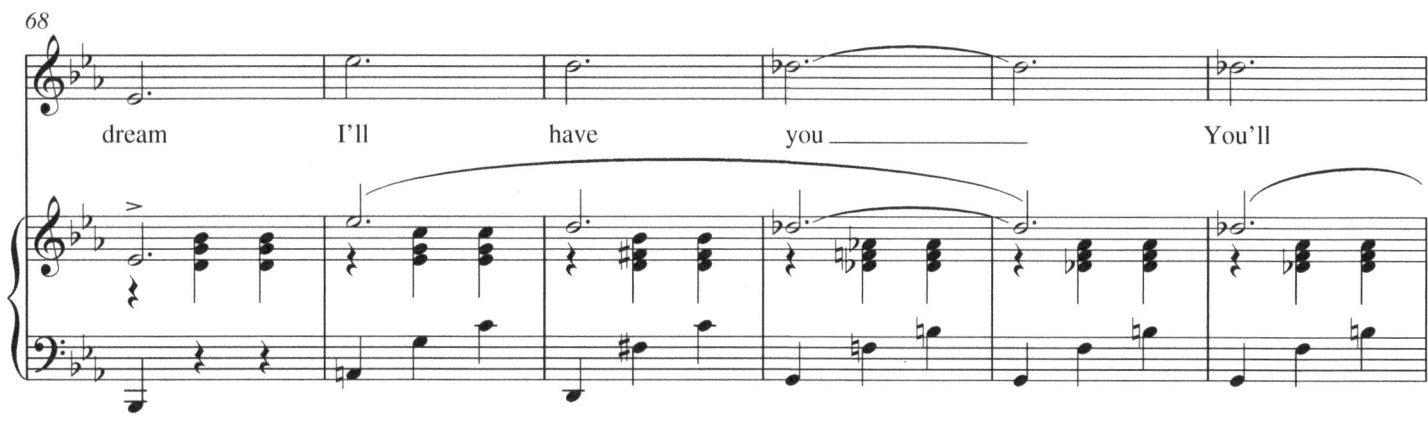
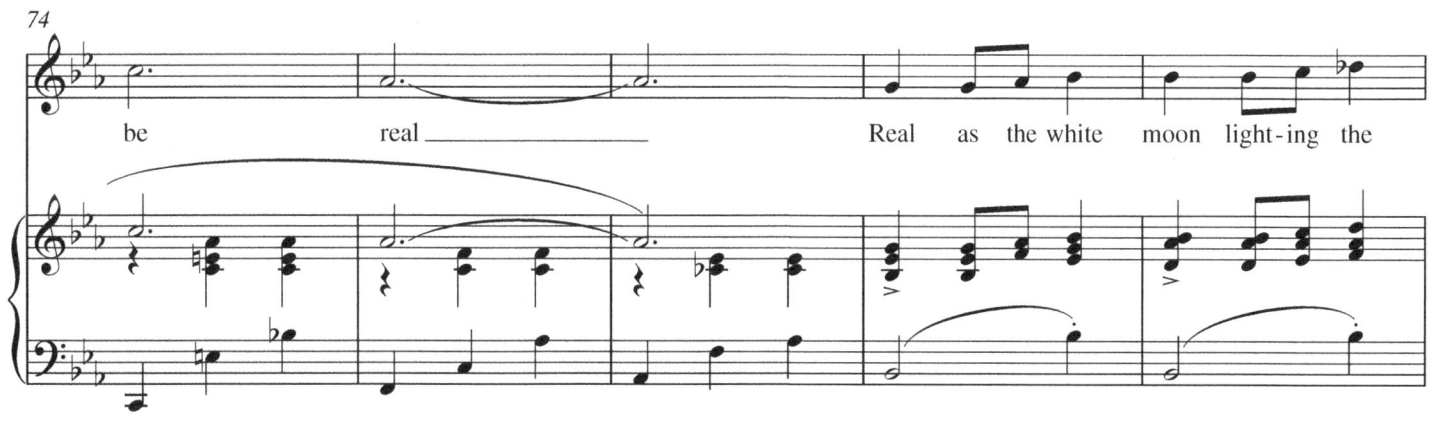

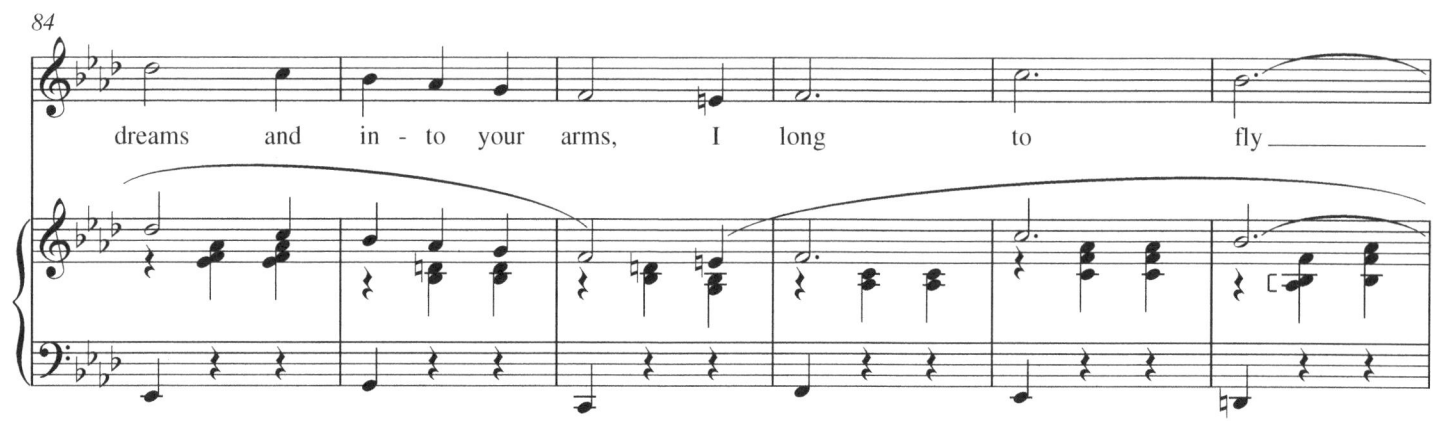
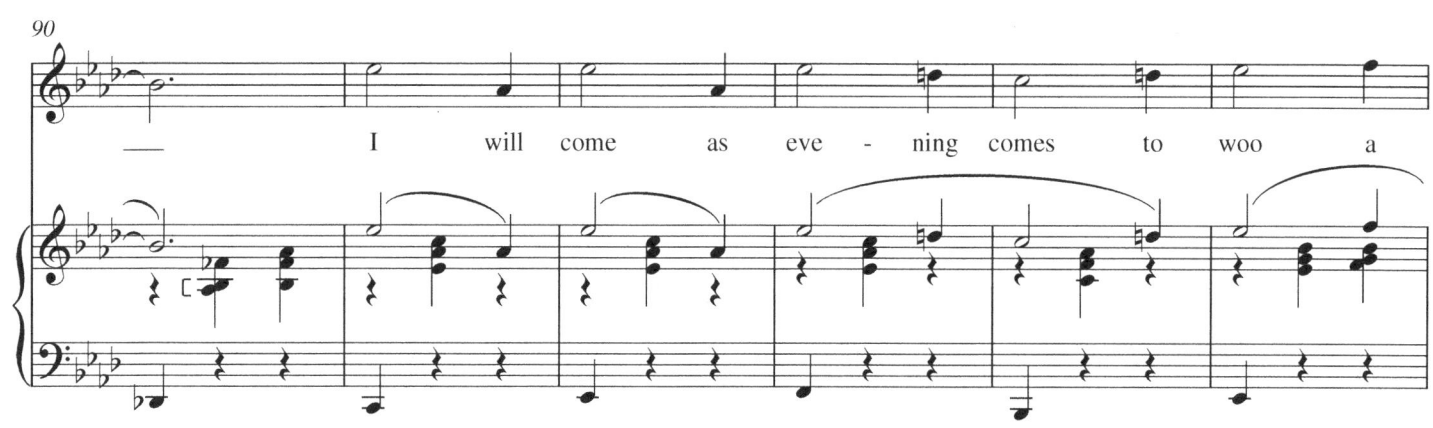

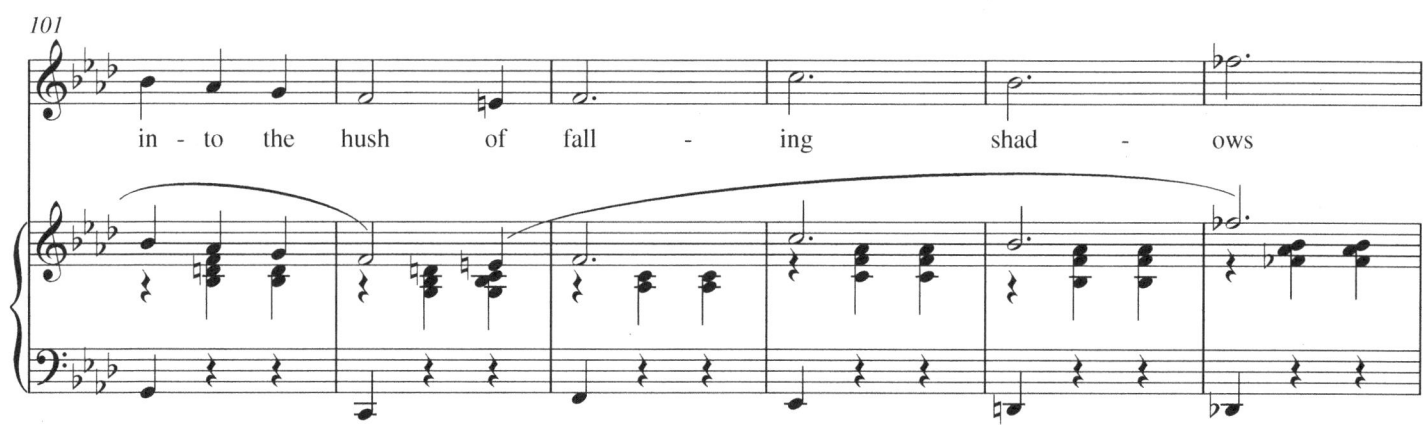

# THIS PLACE IS MINE

from *Phantom*

Words and Music by
Maury Yeston

Copyright © 1991 Yeston Music Ltd. (BMI)
Worldwide Rights for Yeston Music Ltd. Administered by Cherry River Music Co.
International Copyright Secured   All Rights Reserved

# THINK OF ME
from *The Phantom of the Opera*

Music by Andrew Lloyd Webber
Lyrics by Charles Hart
Additional Lyrics by Richard Stilgoe

© Copyright 1986 Andrew Lloyd Webber licensed to The Really Useful Group Ltd.
International Copyright Secured   All Rights Reserved

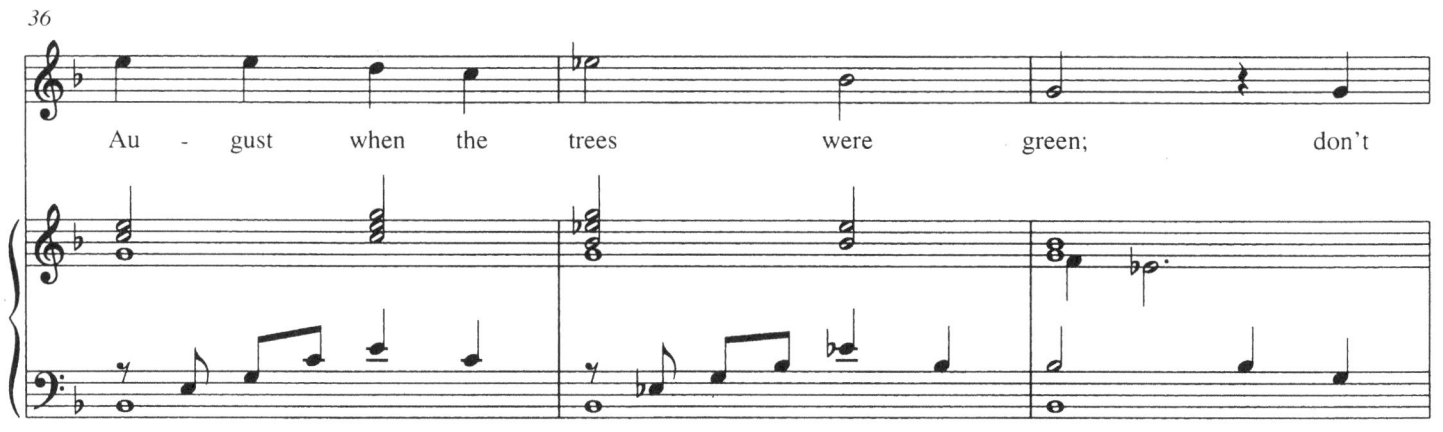

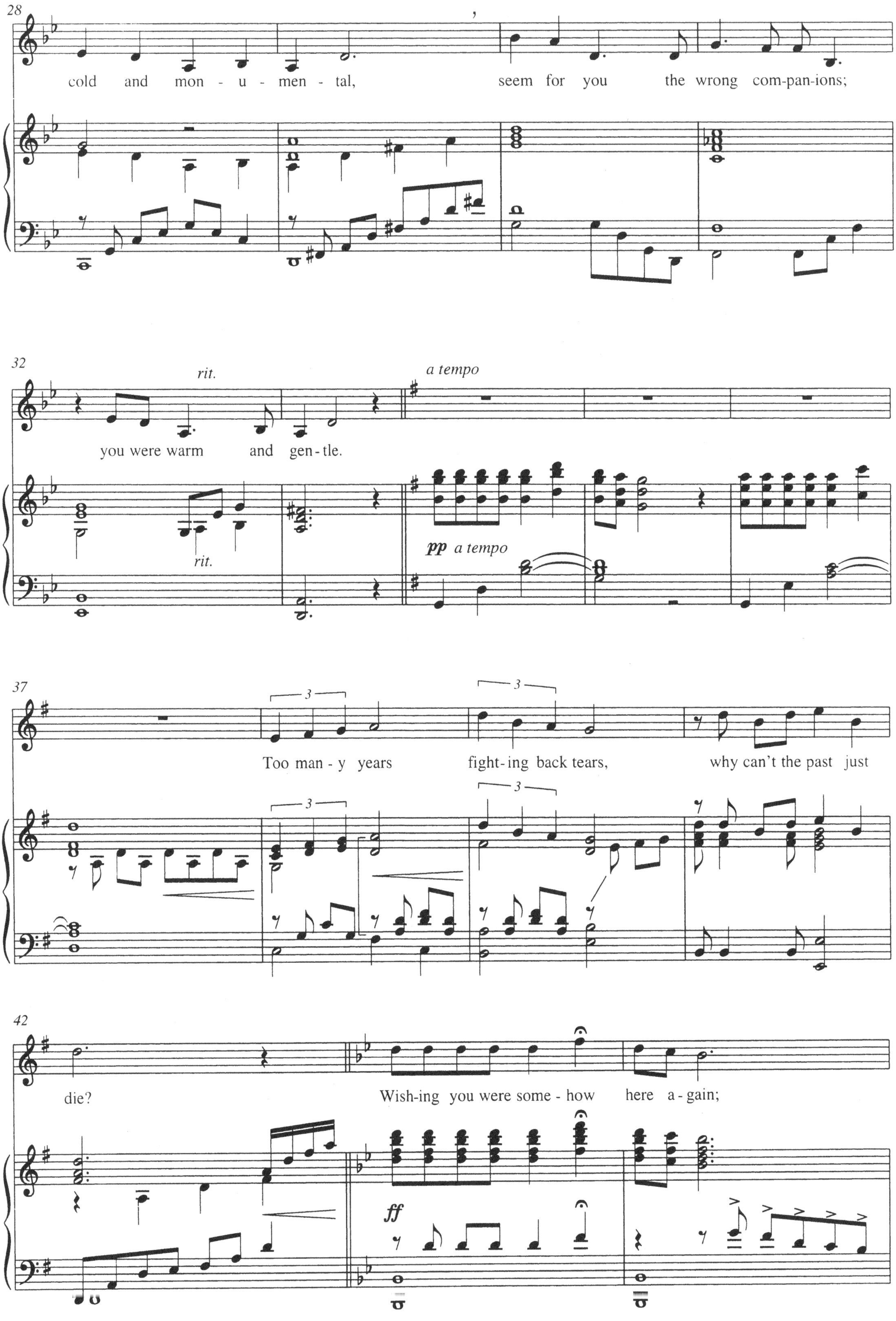
28
cold and mon - u - men - tal,
seem for you the wrong com-pan-ions;
32
rit.
a tempo
you were warm and gen-tle.
pp a tempo
rit.
37
Too man - y years
fight-ing back tears,
why can't the past just
42
die?
Wish-ing you were some - how here a - gain;
ff

# WILL HE LIKE ME?
## from *She Loves Me*

Words by Sheldon Harnick
Music by Jerry Bock

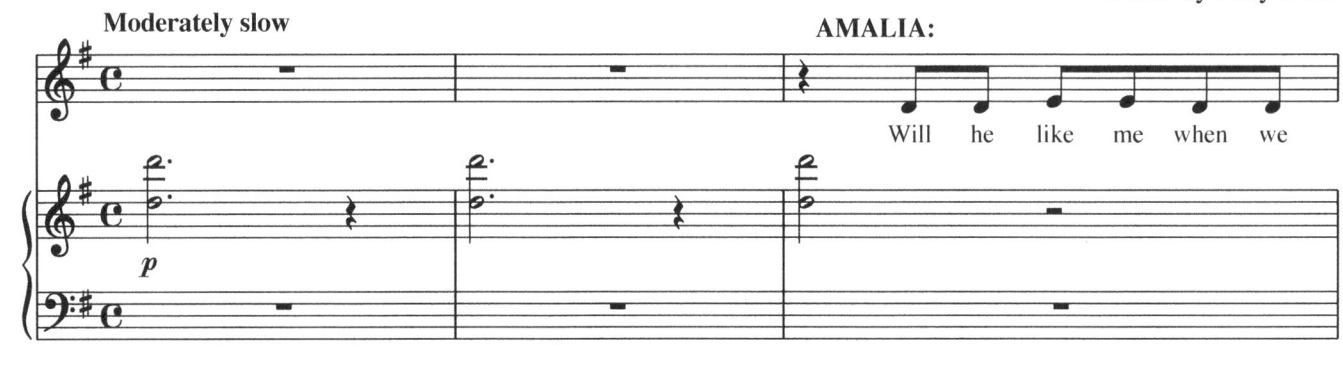
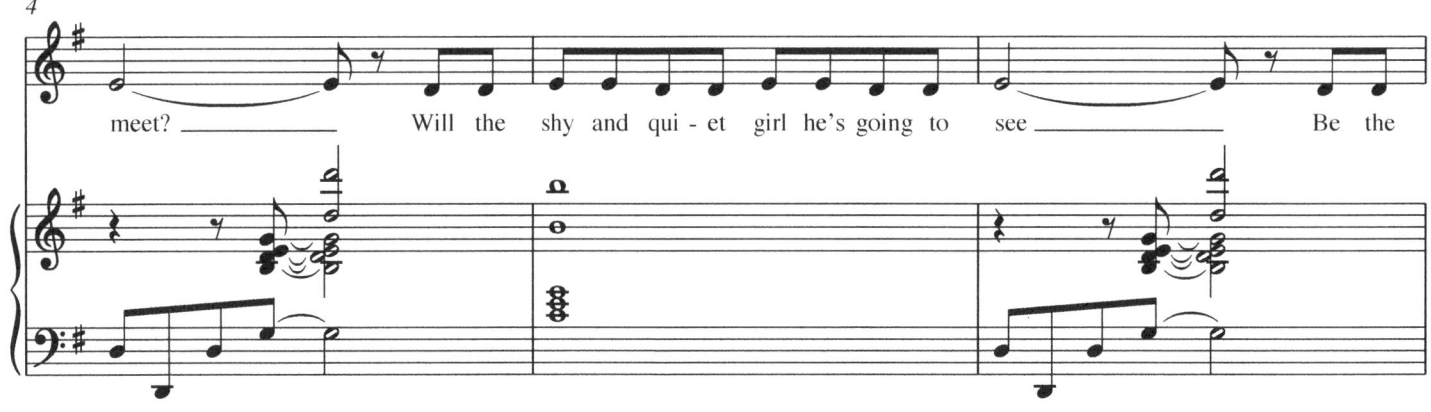
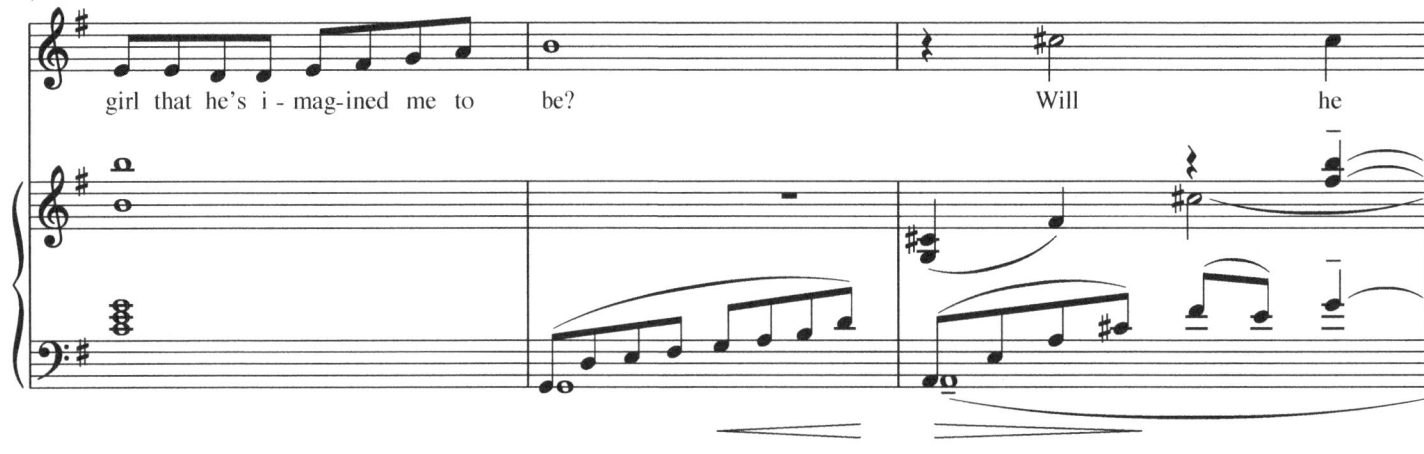

Copyright © 1963 Bock IP LLC and Mayerling Productions, Ltd.
Copyright Renewed 1991
All Rights for Mayerling Productions, Ltd. Administered by R&H Music
International Copyright Secured   All Rights Reserved

# DEAR FRIEND
from *She Loves Me*

Words by Sheldon Harnick
Music by Jerry Bock

Copyright © 1963 Bock IP LLC and Mayerling Productions, Ltd.
Copyright Renewed 1991
All Rights for Mayerling Productions, Ltd. Administered by R&H Music
International Copyright Secured   All Rights Reserved

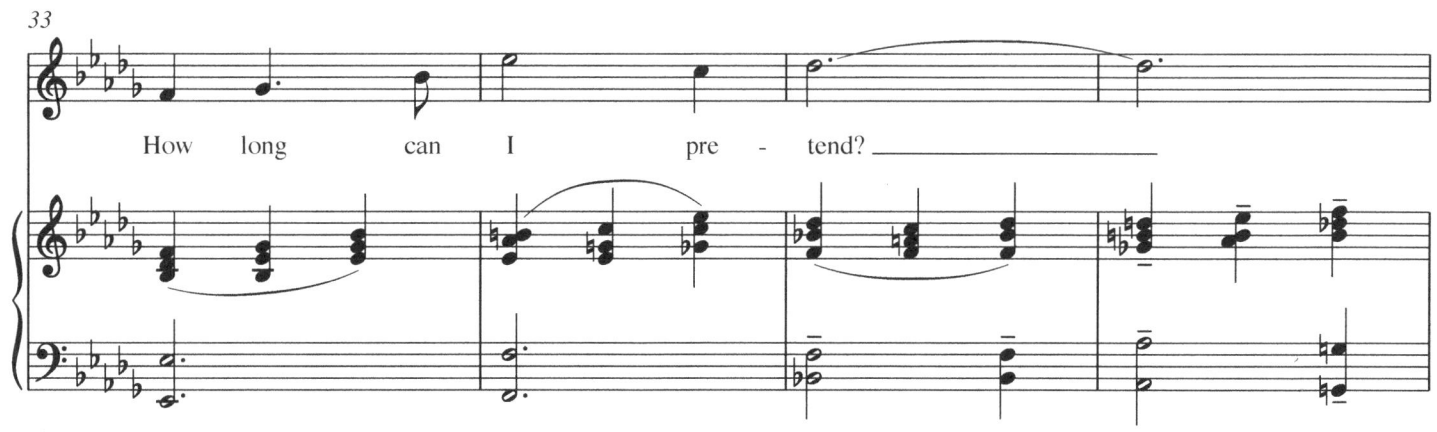

# VANILLA ICE CREAM
## from *She Loves Me*

Words by Sheldon Harnick  
Music by Jerry Bock

# MAKE BELIEVE
## from *Show Boat*

Lyrics by Oscar Hammerstein II
Music by Jerome Kern

*This song is a duet for Magnolia and Ravenal in the show, adapted as a solo for this edition.*

Copyright © 1927 UNIVERSAL - POLYGRAM INTERNATIONAL PUBLISHING, INC.
Copyright Renewed
All Rights Reserved   Used by Permission

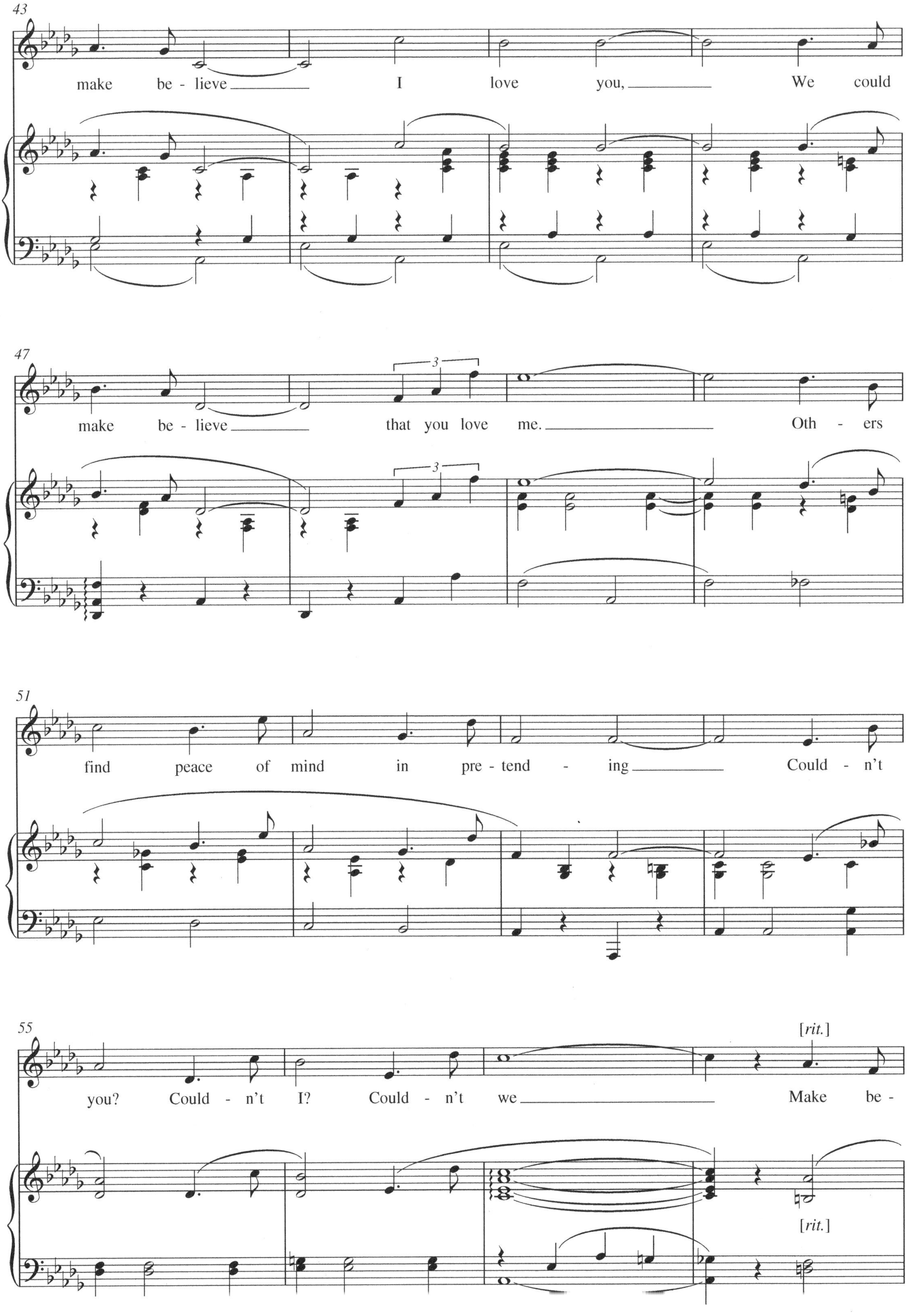
43
make be - lieve I love you, We could
47
make be - lieve that you love me. Oth - ers
3
51
find peace of mind in pre - tend - ing Could - n't
55
you? Could - n't I? Could - n't we Make be -
[rit.]
[rit.]

# CAN'T HELP LOVIN' DAT MAN
from *Show Boat*

Lyrics by Oscar Hammerstein II
Music by Jerome Kern

JULIE: Oh, lis-ten sis-ter, I love my mis-ter man___ And I can't___

___ tell yo' why.___ Dere ain't no rea-son Why I should love dat

*The original dialect in the lyric, printed here, may be adapted in performance to standard English.*

Copyright © 1927 UNIVERSAL - POLYGRAM INTERNATIONAL PUBLISHING, INC.
Copyright Renewed
All Rights Reserved   Used by Permission

* This note presented as originally composed, has been changed in performance tradition to F rather than E-flat. The same is true for measures 32 and 48.

*The editor suggests the higher notes only on the repeat

# BILL
## from *Show Boat*

Music by Jerome Kern
Words by P.G. Wodehouse
and Oscar Hammerstein II

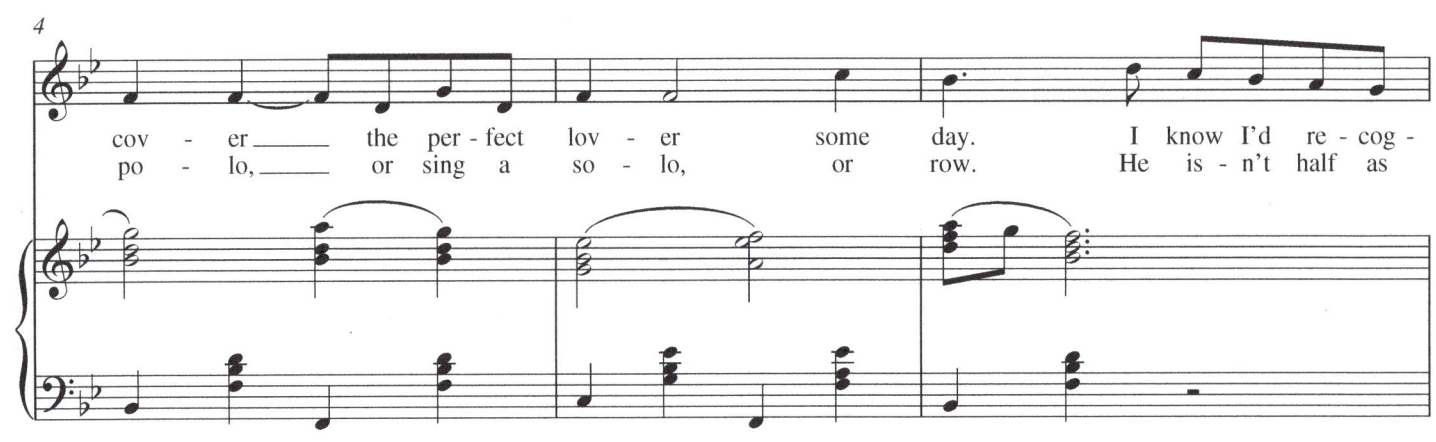

Copyright © 1927 UNIVERSAL - POLYGRAM INTERNATIONAL PUBLISHING, INC.
Copyright Renewed
All Rights Reserved   Used by Permission

# THE SOUND OF MUSIC
## from *The Sound of Music*

Lyrics by Oscar Hammerstein II
Music by Richard Rodgers

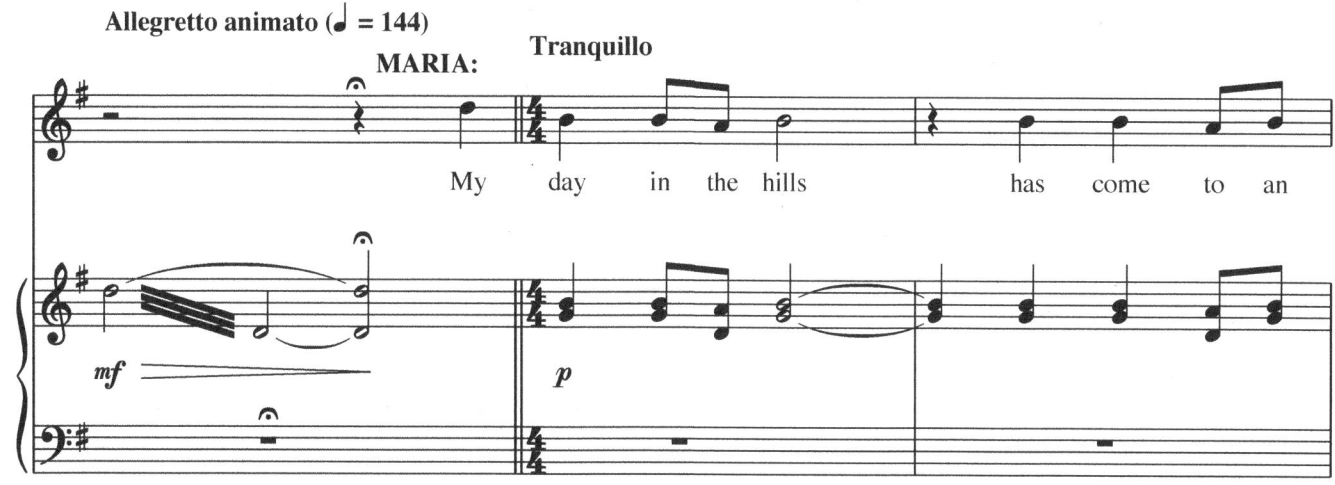

Copyright © 1959 by Richard Rodgers and Oscar Hammerstein II
Copyright Renewed
WILLIAMSON MUSIC owner of publication and allied rights throughout the world
International Copyright Secured   All Rights Reserved

*The optional high note is an editorial suggestion for consideration.*

# Take Care of This House
from *1600 Pennsylvania Avenue*

Lyrics by Alan Jay Lerner
Music by Leonard Bernstein

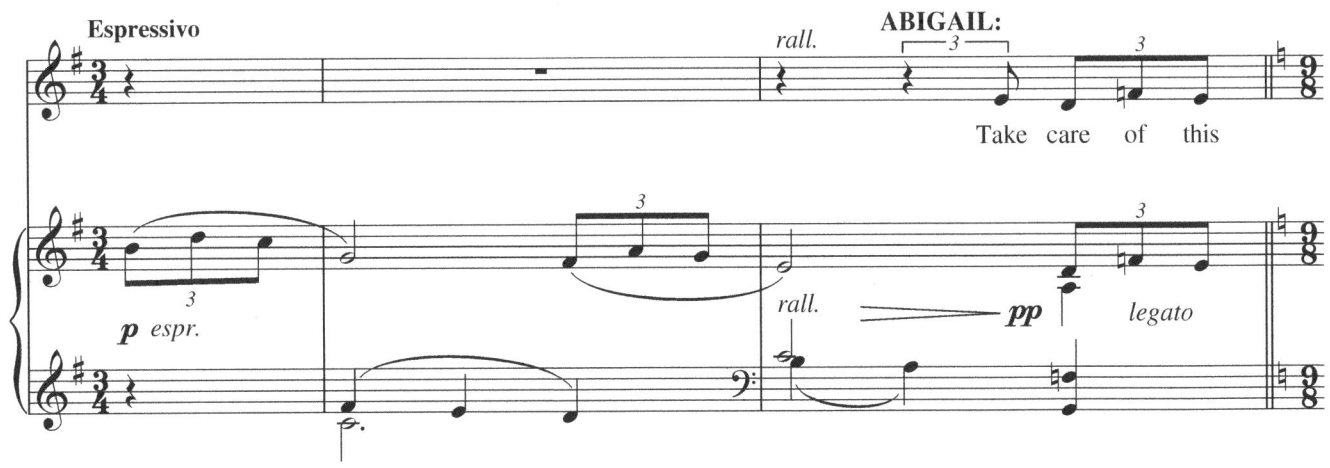

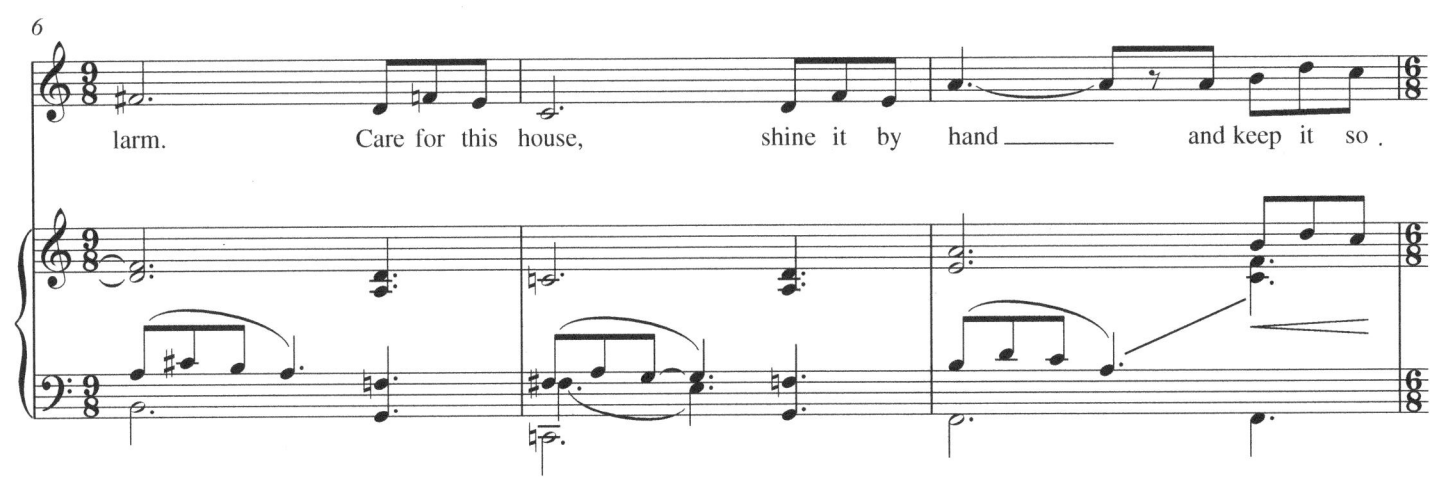

*Originally a duet for Abigail and Lud, this song has been adapted as a solo for this edition.*

© Copyright 1976 by Alan Jay Lerner and Amberson Holdings LLC
Copyright Renewed
Published by Leonard Bernstein Music Publishing Company LLC, as administrator for Leonard Bernstein Music Publishing Company LLC and Ayjayel Music, Inc.
Boosey & Hawkes, Inc., Sole Agent
Copyright for All Countries  All Rights Reserved

# WHAT GOOD WOULD THE MOON BE?

from the Musical Production *Street Scene*

Words by Langston Hughes
Music by Kurt Weill

TRO - © Copyright 1946 (Renewed) Hampshire House Publishing Corp., New York and Chappell & Co., Los Angeles, CA
International Copyright Secured
All Rights Reserved Including Public Performance For Profit
Used by Permission

# GREEN FINCH AND LINNET BIRD
from *Sweeney Todd*

Words and Music by
Stephen Sondheim

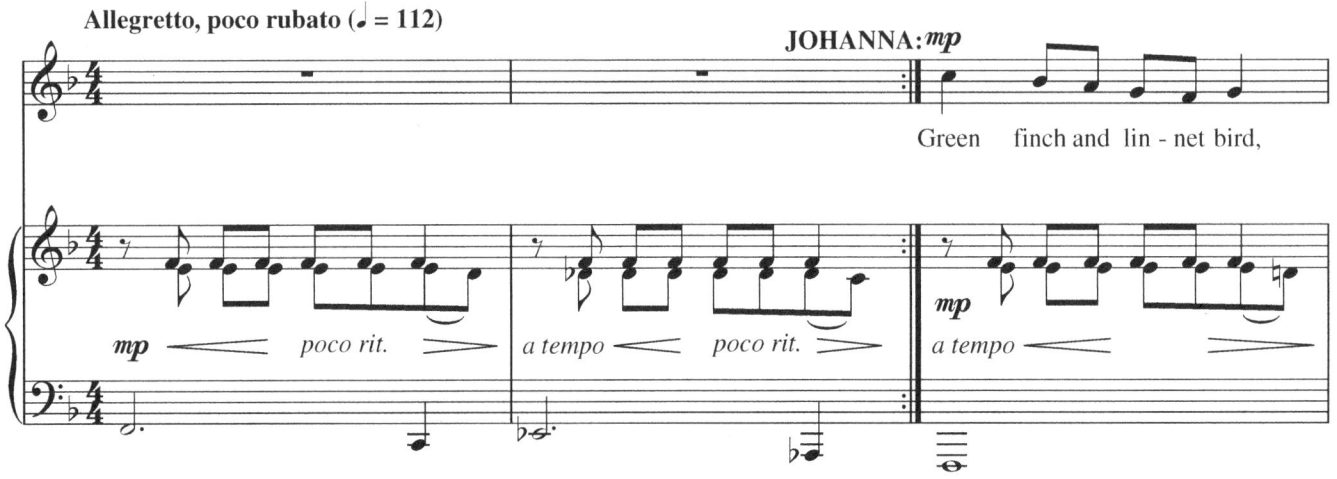

© 1978 RILTING MUSIC, INC.
All Rights Administered by WB MUSIC CORP.
All Rights Reserved   Used by Permission

# I FEEL PRETTY
## from *West Side Story*

Lyrics by Stephen Sondheim
Music by Leonard Bernstein

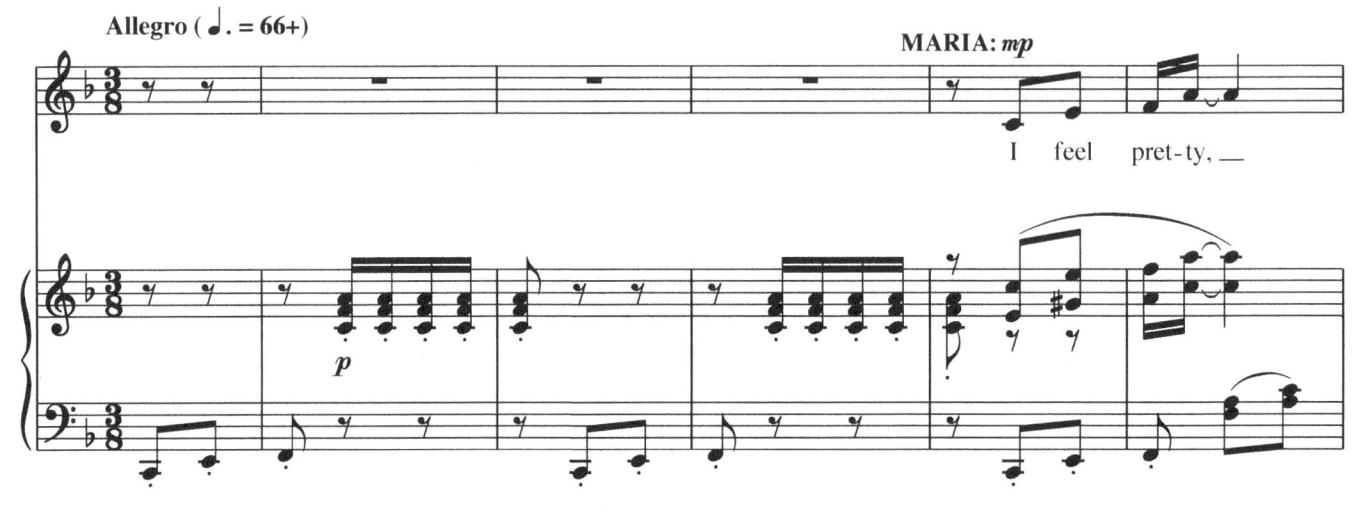

*This scene for Maria, Francisca, Rosalia and Consuelo has been adapted as a solo for this edition.*

Copyright © 1957 by Amberson Holdings LLC and Stephen Sondheim
Copyright Renewed
Leonard Bernstein Music Publishing Company LLC, Publisher
Boosey & Hawkes, Inc., Sole Agent
Copyright For All Countries  All Rights Reserved

# SOMEWHERE
## from *West Side Story*

Lyrics by Stephen Sondheim
Music by Leonard Bernstein

*In the show the song is sung by a character simply known as "A Girl."*

Copyright © 1957 by Amberson Holdings LLC and Stephen Sondheim
Copyright Renewed
Leonard Bernstein Music Publishing Company LLC, Publisher
Boosey & Hawkes, Inc., Sole Agent
Copyright for All Countries   All Rights Reserved

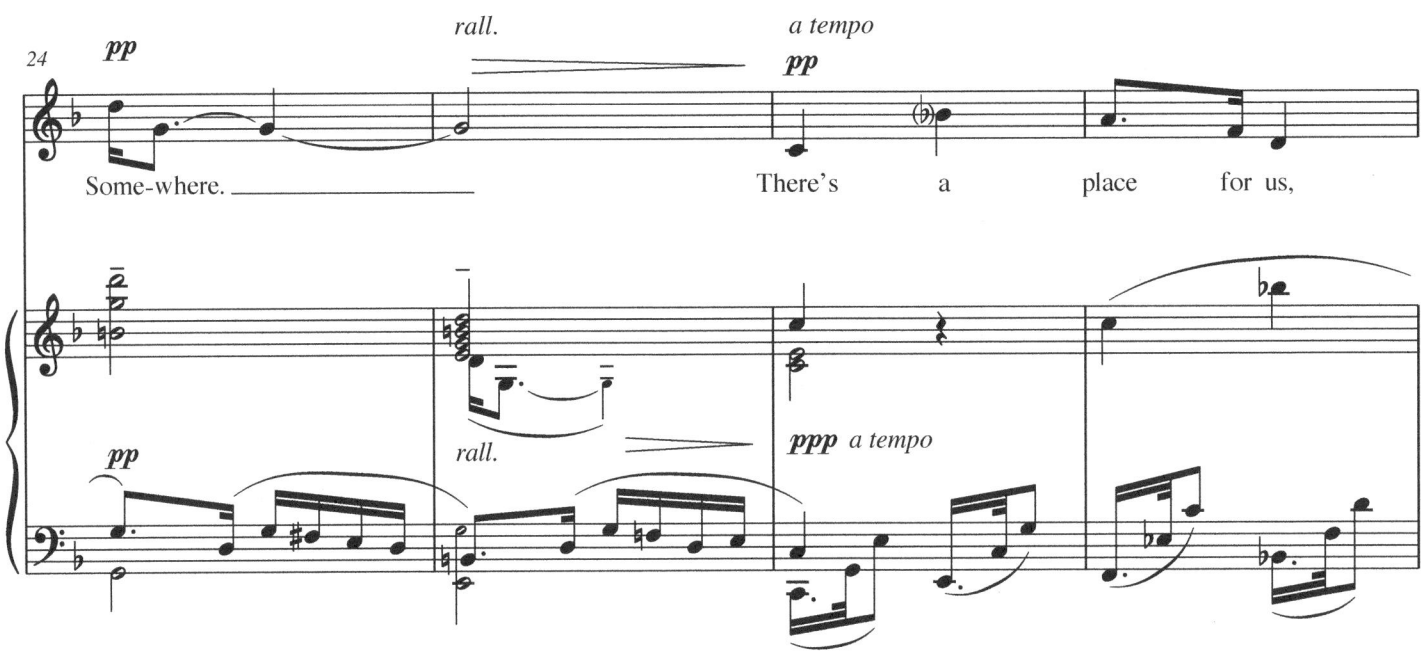

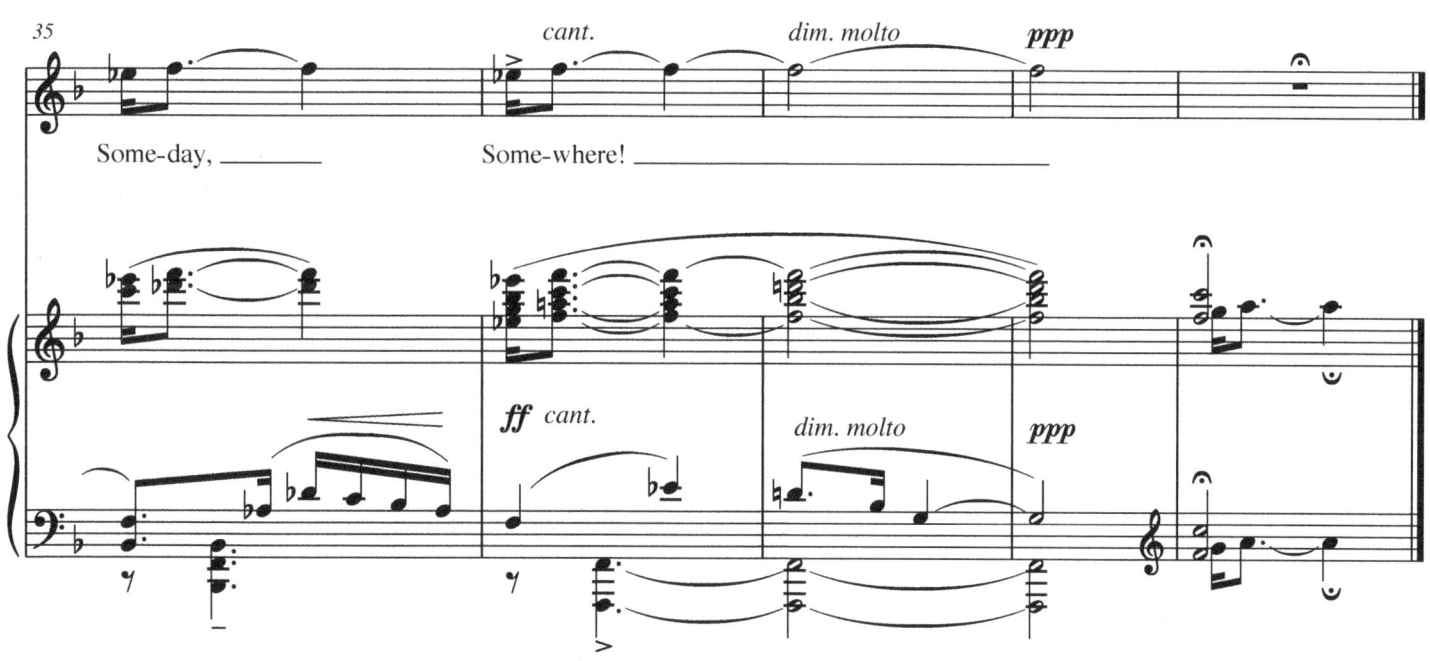

# LET US BE GLAD
## from the Broadway Musical *Wicked*

Music and Lyrics by
Stephen Schwartz

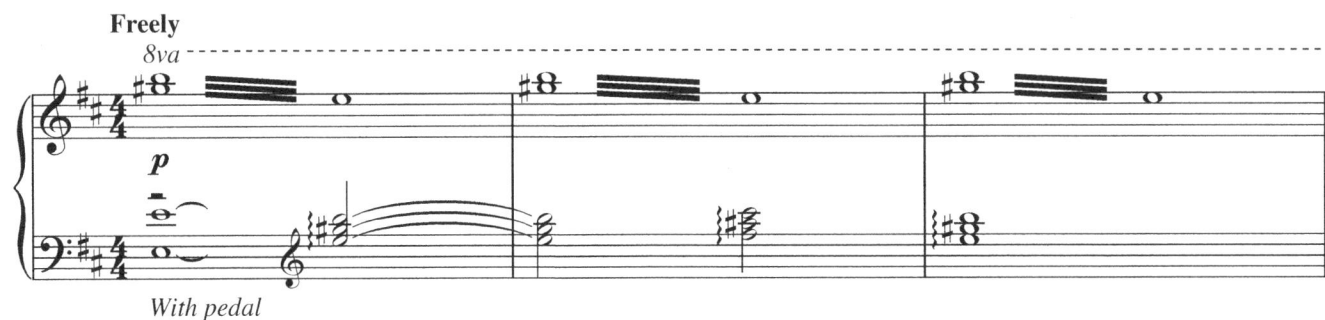

Copyright © 2003 Greydog Music
All Rights Reserved   Used by Permission